RETROSPECT

OF

WESTERN TRAVEL

BY

HARRIET MARTINEAU

IN THREE VOLUMES.

VOL. I.

GREENWOOD PRESS, PUBLISHERS
NEW YORK

Originally published in 1838
by Saunders and Otley, London

First Greenwood Reprinting, 1969

Library of Congress Catalogue Card Number 68-57623

PREFACE.

WHEN I finished my late work on Society in America, I had not the most remote idea of writing any thing more on the subject of the New World. I have since been strongly solicited to communicate more of my personal narrative, and of the lighter characteristics of men, and incidents of travel, than it suited my purpose to give in the other work. It has also been represented to me that, as my published book concerns the Americans at least as much as the English, there is room for another which shall supply to the English what the Americans do not want,—a picture of the aspect of the country, and of its men and manners. There seems no reason why such a picture should not be appended to an inquiry into the theory and practice of their

society: especially as I believe that I have
little to tell which will not strengthen the
feelings of respect and kindness with which
the people of Great Britain are more and
more learning to regard the inhabitants of
the Western Republic. I have therefore willingly acceded to the desire of such of my
readers as have requested to be presented
with my Retrospect of Western Travel.

H. M.

CONTENTS OF VOL. I.

	Page
The Voyage	1
First Impressions	42
The Hudson	55
Pine Orchard House	81
Weddings	92
High Road Travelling	106
Fort Erie	140
Niagara	151
Priestley	175
Prisons	199
First Sight of Slavery	228
Life at Washington	235
The Capitol	274
Mount Vernon	311

RETROSPECT

OF

WESTERN TRAVEL.

THE VOYAGE.

"When the sun dawned, gay and glad,
We set the sail and plied the oar;
But when the night-wind blew like breath,
For joy of one day's voyage more,
We sang together on the wide sea,
Like men at peace on a peaceful shore;
Each sail was loosed to the wind so free,
The helm made sure by the twilight star,
And in a sleep as calm as death
We the voyagers from afar
Lay stretched . . . . ."

Paracelsus, Part iv.

THE packet-ship in which my passage was taken, the United States, Captain Nathan Holdrege, was to have sailed from Liverpool on Friday the 8th of August, 1834, at eleven o'clock. At half-past ten, my fellow-traveller and I, with our friends, were on the way to the dock, in some doubt about our departure, from the wind being directly against us, when we met a gentleman interested in the sailing of the vessel, who told us that we might turn back, as the Captain had given up all hope of getting out of port that day. This was uncomfortable news enough. We had bidden farewell to many friends, half the pain of parting was over, and there was little pleasure in having it all to go through again.

We resolved to proceed to the dock, to put our luggage on board, and see for ourselves the true state of affairs. It was not very agreeable. The deck was encumbered with water-casks and chests; the Captain was fidgetting about, giving his orders in a voice rather less placid than ordinary; a great number of inquiring persons, who had come down to see us off, had to be told that we were not going to-day, and why; and several of the American passengers were on the spot, looking very melancholy. They had entered the 8th in their journals as the day of sailing, brought down their portmanteaus, paid their bills at the hotel, and taken leave of Boots and chambermaid. Here they were left with four-and-twenty dreary and expensive hours upon their hands—and who knew how many more than four-and-twenty? One declared that the wind appeared as if it had set in against us, and he should not be surprised if it was a week before we sailed. Their fate was so truly mournful, that I was ashamed of feeling any discomfiture on my own account, domesticated as I was in the nearest and dearest of homes, next to my own. Our disconsolate acquaintance among the passengers were invited to dispose of their evening with us; and we returned, to tell the children, and everybody whom we met, that we were not gone, and wherefore. Of course, we presently recollected several reasons why it was well that we had another day. There were two letters which it was highly desirable I should write from Liverpool rather than from New York; and the children had never before found leisure to show me the cupboards and shelves where they kept their playthings; so that if the wind had been fair, I should actually have gone away without seeing them.

We sauntered all the afternoon in the Zoological Gardens, and as we returned, caught each other looking up at every weathercock we passed. In the evening, our visitors dropped in, each ready with a speculation as to how the wind would be to-morrow.

On the morrow, the weathercock told no better news; and a note was on the breakfast-table which informed us that there was no chance of our sailing that day. I was now really sorry. It was Saturday; and I feared my host would write no sermon if I remained to keep his household in an unsettled state. Our sea dresses, too, would not serve for a Sunday in Liverpool, and our books and work were all on board, with our wardrobes. The tidings were therefore welcome which were brought early

in the forenoon, that the Captain had engaged a
steam-boat to tow us out to sea. By eleven o'clock
the carriage of a friend was at the door, with bou-
quets of flowers, and baskets of grapes and other
acid refreshments, which it was thought might be
welcome at sea.

" Have you *no* misgivings?" asked an intimate,
before whose imagination the Western World now
rose tremendous in its magnitude. " Have you no
misgivings now?" I had none, and it was well. If
I had had such as would have made me draw back
at the last moment, what a world of good should I
have foregone! Not only what knowledge,—but
what a store of imagery! What intense and varied
enjoyment! and, above all, what friendships! When
I now look back upon what I have gained, and at
how small an expense of peril and inconvenience, I
cannot but regard my setting foot on board ship as
one of the most fortunate acts of my life.

When we arrived at the dock, we found there was
really to be no further delay. The knots of friends,
the crowds of gazers were gathering; the steamer
was hissing and puffing in the river, and the song of
the sailors was heard, as they were warping our ship
out of the dock. In a few minutes, we and the
other passengers were requested to step on board.
I first carried my flowers down to my state-room,
intending to hide them there till we should be out

of sight of land, when an apparition of fresh flowers
upon deck might be more than commonly welcome.
I then took my station by a window of the round-
house, whence I could see all that passed on shore,
without being much seen. Thence I could observe
my brother and sisters speaking to each other, and
pointing out things which I could easily interpret.
It occurred to me that I could send them one more
token, by means of the little waves which rolled
away from the sides of our ship, and washed the
pier on which the crowd was standing. I threw out
a rose at a moment when I caught a watchful eye;
and I saw it borne, after many vagaries, directly
under their feet. Suddenly I missed them from the
spot where they were standing, and supposed that
they were quite tired, (as they well might have
been,) and had gone home. But it was not so.
They had withdrawn only in order to secure front
places at the extreme end of the pier, whence they
might watch us yet longer than from their former
station. There they stood, as long as we could dis-
tinguish any forms from among the crowd. Then
three cheers were exchanged between the crew and
the shore, and the passengers strained their eyes no
more.

The greater number then went below, to make
arrangements in their state-rooms; and afterwards
ensued the ceremony of introducing the company

to each other on deck. Our number was twenty-three, six of whom formed the party to which I belonged : or rather so it seemed to ourselves before we went on board. The distinction was afterwards forgotten, for the company assembled was, with two or three exceptions, so exceedingly agreeable, and so wonderfully congenial, considering how accidentally we were brought together, that we mingled completely as one party. We had among us a Prussian physician; a New England divine; a Boston merchant, with his sprightly and showy young wife; a high-spirited young South Carolinian, fresh from a German University; a newly-married couple, whose station was not exactly discoverable while on board, but who opened a public-house soon after their arrival in New York; a Scotch major, whose peculiarities made him the butt of the young men; an elderly widow lady; two amiable young ladies; and a Scotch lady, " of no particular age," but of very particular placidity and good humour; and a youth out of Yorkshire, who was leaving his parents' roof for the first time alone, and who was destined never to return to it. The number was made up by English and American merchants—young men so accustomed to pass between Liverpool and New York, that the voyage was little more to them than an expedition to Primrose Hill is to a cockney.

The cold dinner, and drinking of healths, cus-

tomary on the day of sailing, succeeded. Then
there was the library to look over, and trial to be
made of a seat on the rail, whence we could see the
dim shores, as we glided smoothly along in the
wake of the steamer. By the time it was dusk, the
latter had performed her engagement. We saw the
payment handed over, and the shaking of hands of
the two captains, and then she disengaged herself
from us, and began ploughing her way to the north
coast of Ireland. We felt very helpless when she
was gone, the little wind there was being unfavourable. There was so little, however, as to allow us
novices a night of sound sleep at the outset.

On Sunday, we crept along in almost a calm, having a glimpse of the dim outline of the Isle of Man
in the morning, and being still in sight of Holyhead
in the evening. To me, it was a day of luxury;
for, jaded as I had been with business and novelty,
there was no circumstance of the voyage that I
valued so highly as the impossibility of receiving
letters or news for three weeks or a month. The
gliding on thus in a calm, with time to think and be
still, was all that I wanted: but the Americans,
who had home on the horizon before them, and
longed to be at rest there, looked grave on this in-
auspicious beginning of their transit. On Monday,
however, they felt, from another cause, a good deal
worse. The wind had freshened; but I believe

nobody cared which way, or how fast, it blew us. The only meal at which I was not present was that Monday's dinner. I can testify to the breakfast and tea being quiet and sad enough, with a sprinkling of languid passengers at table, and a knowledge of how wretched all the rest were in their rooms.

On Tuesday began my experience of the pleasures of the sea. The wind had freshened to a strong breeze, which had so rocked us in our berths that I rose miserably ill. I was strongly persuaded of the necessity of exertion in sea-sickness, of having fresh air, and of getting out of the way of the sights and sounds of the cabin; and I therefore persevered in dressing and going up to the deck. There was the captain, with only one passenger to talk with, and heartily glad at the prospect of another being convalescent. He seated me on the rail, where I kept my eyes away from the helpless invalids who were strewed about the deck: and in half an hour I was quite well. We were careering along in most exhilarating style. The wind was so strong as to put the wearing a bonnet out of the question. I had happily been furnished with a sort of cap which no lady should go to sea without;—a black silk cap, well wadded. With the head thus defended, and a large warm cloak, a lady may abide almost any weather, and avoid the *désagrémens* and unwholesomeness of the cabin. My eye was never weary of watching the dashing and boiling of the dark green waves, from the grey horizon to the ship's side; and I know of no motion so gladsome as that of riding the high billows in a brisk breeze. The captain pointed out to me the first of the monsters of the deep that I ever saw;—a large black-fish, tumbling about joyously by itself in the stormy sea, now throwing its thick body forward in ungainly gambols, and now rearing its forked tail perpendicularly, as it prepared to dive.

My flowers did not disappoint my expectations. They were still quite fresh on the Wednesday, when, as we were out of sight of land, I carried them up to the deck, and gave each passenger one, —that being precisely my supply. I never saw flowers give so much pleasure before, except in cases of long confinement from illness. Truly they were very like a message from home.

In two or three days more, all but two ladies and one gentleman had settled themselves into the routine of sea life. It was very desirable that they should do so, as on the 15th we were still little more than 300 miles from Liverpool. It would have been dismal to add idleness and unsettledness to the discouragement caused by such a beginning of our voyage. Our mode of life was very simple and quiet: to me, very delightful. I enjoyed it so much that I delayed beginning my letters home till we

had been a week at sea, lest I should write some
extravagance which I should afterwards have to
qualify or retract.   None of my subsequent experience, however, has altered my feeling that a voyage
is the most pleasant pastime I have ever known.

The passengers showed themselves upon deck
some time between seven and nine in the morning.
Each one either made his way to the binnacle, to see
for himself what course we were upon, or learned
the important intelligence from some obliging individual who held the fact at the general service.
We all asked the captain at first : but soon discon-
tinued the practice, when we found that favourable
answers were likely to be rare, and how it must vex
him to tell us every morning that we were scarcely
getting on at all.

After a brisk morning's walk upon deck, no one
was sorry to hear the breakfast bell.   Breakfast
was the most cheerful meal of the day.   If ever
there was any news to tell, it was then.   The early
risers could sometimes speak to the sluggards of a
big fish, of a passing sail, of a frolic among the
sailors.   I was asked once by a passenger, in a tone
whose laziness cannot be conveyed on paper, " What,
did ye see the whale this mornin' ? "

" No.   It came at four o'clock, when I was
asleep : but the captain promises to have me called
next time, whatever the hour may be."

" What, d'ye want to see a whale ?"

" Yes, very much."

" Well, but I dare say you have seen a pictur' o' one."

It was not apparent to him that this was not an equally good thing.

After breakfast, the gentlemen who kept journals produced their writing cases in the cabin. The ladies sat in sunny or shaded places on deck, netting, making table-mats, or reading; or mounted the rail to talk or look abroad. I had a task to do; which is a thing that should be avoided on board ship. I had a long article to write; and nothing else would I do, on fine mornings, till it was finished. It is disagreeable writing in the cabin, with people flitting all about one. It is unwholesome writing in one's state-room, in the month of August. The deck is the only place. The first care after breakfast, of my clerical friend, the New Englander, was to find me a corner where the wind would not blow my paper about, where the sun would not dazzle me, and where I might be quiet: and then he took his seat behind the round-house, with a row of children from the steerage before him, to do their lessons. I wondered at first how he would teach them without books, slates, or any other visible implements of instruction : but when I saw him get a potato, and cut it into two and four

parts, to show the children what halves and quarters
were, I was assured he would prosper with them.
And so he did. They went to school to excellent
purpose ; and I dare say they will send back
grateful thoughts, all through their lives, upon the
kind gentleman who attended to them on the
voyage.

For some time I was daily baffled in my purpose of writing by the observation of persons who
seemed not only entirely ignorant of the process of
composition, but very anxious to learn it. Not
only did the children from the steerage spy from
behind chests and casks, and peep over my shoulder,
but the inquirer about the whale was wont to place
himself directly in front of me, with his arms
akimbo, and his eyes fixed on the point of my pen.
Somebody gave him a hint at last, and I was left in
peace. By two o'clock, when the deck began to
fill again after luncheon, my head and eyes had had
enough of writing, and I joyfully mounted the rail.
If I wanted to watch the sea undisturbed, I held
a Shakspeare in my hand. If I carried no book,
somebody came to talk. What fleets of Portuguese
men-of-war did we see at those hours ! I hardly
know whether these little mariners of the deep are
most beautiful when gliding, rich in their violet
hues, along the calm sunny surface of the summer
sea, or when they are tossed about, like toys, by

rough dark waves. One day, when I was exclaiming on their beauty, a young lady, industriously working at her table-mats, observed that it was very odd that she had crossed this ocean three times, and had never seen a Portuguese man-of-war. I concluded that she had never looked for them, and asked the favour of her to stand by my side for one half hour. She did so, and saw three. I strongly suspect that those who complain of the monotony of the ocean, do not use their eyes as they do on land. It seems to be the custom at sea to sit on deck, looking abroad only when the sun is setting, or the moon rising, or when there is a sail to be speculated upon. Some of the most beautiful sights I caught were when no one else was looking down quite into the deep—the only way to see most of the creatures that live there. One day I was startled, while thus gazing, with an exquisite radiance, like an expanse of brilliant rainbow, far down in the sunny deep under our bows. My exclamation brought one witness to behold, as I did, the distinct form of a dolphin come out of the light. It was a family of dolphins,—the only ones that were seen on the voyage. Many a flying fish darted from the crest of one wave into another. Many a minuet did Mother Carey's chickens trip, with their slender web-feet, on the momentary calm left between two billows. Many a shining visitor came up from the

lowest deep, to exchange glances and be gone. I
soon found it was in vain to call people to look.
These sights are too transient to be caught otherwise
than by watching. When a shoal of porpoises
came to race with the ship, every one on board was
up on the rail to see; and an exhilarating sight it
is, when the ship is going before the wind in a rough
sea, and the porpoises dart visibly through the midst
of a billow, and pitch and rise, and cross each
other's path, swiftly and orderly, without ever
relaxing their speed, till they are tired of play. It
is impossible to help having a favourite among the
shoal, and watching him with an interest and
admiration which, upon consideration, are really
ridiculous.

The most generally interesting sight, perhaps, was
a sail; and we were never a day without seeing one
or more. Sometimes three or four seemed to be peeping at us from the horizon. Sometimes our ship and
another were nearing each other almost all day. Once
or twice, I was startled with a sudden apparition of
one close at hand, with all her sails set, black in a
streak of moonlight, when I went up to bid the sea
goodnight. One morning early, I found the deck
in a bustle, from a ship having made signals of
distress. " A ship in distress!" every body began
shouting. " A ship in distress!" cried I to the
ladies in the cabin, one of whom came up muffled

in a cloak, and another with her nightcap under her bonnet, rather than miss the romance of the scene. The hearts of the novices were all ready to bleed; the faces of the gentlemen began to wear, in anticipation, an expression of manly compassion, as we hung out our colours, shortened sail (one of the first times we had been going right on our course), and wore round, while all the people of both ships gathered on the decks, and the captains brandished their trumpets. She was French, and her distress was that she had lost her longitude! Our good captain, very angry at the loss of time from such a cause, said they ought to have lost their heads with it, shouted out the longitude, and turned into our course again. The ladies went back to finish their toilette in an ordinary mood of sensibility, and the French went on their way, we may conclude, rejoicing.

A distant sail was one day decided to be a merchant ship from the south of France,—to everybody's apparent satisfaction but mine. I had a strong persuasion that she was not French, but felt how presumptuous it would be to say so. I watched her, however; and at the end of three hours, directed the captain's attention again to her. He snatched his glass, and the next moment electrified us all by the vehemence of his directions to the helmsman, and others of the crew. It was a rival

packet-ship, the Montreal, which had left Ports-
mouth four days before we sailed.   We were in for
a race, which lasted three days, after which we lost
sight of our rival, till she reached New York after
us.   Our captain left the dinner table three times
this first day of the race, and was excessively
anxious throughout.   It was very exciting to us all.
We concluded, after fair trial, that she beat in a
light wind, and we in a strong one.   Some weeks
after our landing, I fell in with two passengers from
the Montreal, who described the counterpart of the
scene we had witnessed as having taken place on
board their ship.   There had been the same start of
surprise on the part of their captain, who had also
left the dinner table three times ; the same excitement among the passengers ; and the same conclu-
sion as to the respective sailing merits of the two
vessels.

From four to six we were dining.   Some of us
felt it rather annoying to be so long at table : but it
is a custom established on board these packets, for
the sake, I believe, of those who happen to find the
day too long.   Such persons need compassion ; and
their happier companions can afford to sacrifice
something to their ease : so no one objects openly to
devoting two of the best hours of the day to dinner
and dessert.   The rush up to the deck, however,
when they are over, shows what the taste of the

majority is. One afternoon the ladies were called down again, and found in their cabin a surprise at least as agreeable as my flowers. A dessert of pines and grapes had been sent in by a gentleman who found that a friend had put a basket of choice fruits on board for his use, but who preferred favouring the ladies with them. He was sent for to preside at the table he had thus spread, and was not a little rallied by his brother passengers on his privileges. These things seem trifles on paper, but they yield no trifling amusement on a voyage. Our afternoons were delightful. For the greater number of the forty-two days that we were at sea, the sun set visibly, with more or less lustre, and all eyes were watching his decline. There was an unusual quietness on board just about sunset. All the cabin passengers were collected on one side, except any two or three who might be in the rigging. The steerage passengers were to be seen looking out at the same sight, and probably engaged as we were in pointing out some particular bar of reddened cloud, or snowy mountain of vapours, or the crimson or golden light spattered on the swelling sides of the billows, as they heaved sunwards. Then came the last moment of expectation,—even to the rising on tip-toe, as if that would enable us to see a spark more of the sun: and then the revival of talk, and the bustle of pairing off to walk. This was the hour for walking the deck; and, till near tea-time, almost the whole company might be seen parading like a school. I never grew very fond of walking on a heaving floor, on which you have to turn at the end of every thirty paces or so: but it is a duty to walk on board ship; and it is best to do it at this hour, and in full and cheerful company.

After tea, the cabin was busy with whist and chess parties, readers, and laughers and talkers. On damp and moonless evenings, I joined a whist party; but my delight was the deck at this time, when I had it all to myself, or when I could at least sit alone in the stern. I know no greater luxury than singing alone in the stern on fine nights, when there is no one within hearing but the helmsman, and sights of beauty meet the eye wherever it turns. Behind, the light from the binnacle alone gleams upon the deck; dim, shifting lights and shadows mark out the full sails against the sky, and stars look down between. The young moon drops silently into the sea afar. In our wake is a long train of pale fire, perpetually renewed as we hiss through the dark waves. On such a quiet night, how startling is a voice from the deck, or a shout of laughter from the cabin! More than once, when I heard the voices of children and the barking of a dog from the steerage, I wholly forgot for the moment that I was at sea, and looking up, was struck breathless at the sight of the dim, grey, limitless expanse. Never, however, did I see the march of the night so beautiful over hill, dale, wood, or plain as over the boundless sea, roofed with its complete arch. The inexpressible silence, the undimmed lustre, the steady visible motion of the sky, make the night what it can nowhere be on land, unless in the midst of the Great Desert, or on a high mountain-top.—It is not the clear still nights alone that are beautiful. Nothing can be more chilling to the imagination than the idea of fog : yet I have seen exquisite sights in a night-fog ;—not in a pervading, durable mist; but in such a fog as is common at sea; thick and driving, with spaces through which the moon may shine down, making clusters of silvery islands on every side. This was an entirely new appearance to me; and the white Archipelago was a spectacle of great beauty. Then again, the action of the ship in a strong night-breeze is fine; cutting her steady way through the seething waters, and dashing them from her sides so uniformly and strongly, that for half a mile on either hand, the sea is as a white marble floor, gemmed with stars ;—just like a child's idea of "the pavement of the heavenly courts." Such are the hours when all that one has ever known or thought that is beautiful comes back softly and mysteriously; snatches of old songs, all one's first loves in poetry and in the phantasmagoria of nature. No sleep is sweeter than that into which one sinks in such a mood, when one's spirit drops anchor amidst the turbulence of the outward world, and the very power of the elements seems to shed stillness into the soul.

There must be many a set off against such hours, however, or the whole world would be rushing to sea. There would be parties to the Azores as there now are to Rome, and people would be doubling the Capes as they now cross the Simplon. There are disagreeable hours and days at sea;—whole days, when the ship rolls so as to stop employment in the cabin; and the rain pours down so as to prevent any weary passenger from putting out his head upon deck; when the captain is to be seen outside in his sea-coat, with the water streaming from nose, chin, hat, and every projection of his costume; when every one's limbs are aching with keeping himself from tumbling over his neighbour; when the tea and coffee are cold, and all that is liquid is spilt, and everything solid thrown out of its place. The best thing to be done on such days is to sit in the round-house, each one well wedged in between two, the balustrade in front, and the wall behind; all as loquacious as possible, talking all manner of sense or nonsense that may occur; those who can joke, joking; those who can sing, singing; those who know any new games teaching them. This is better than the only other thing that can be done,—lying in one's heaving berth; better, not only because it is more sociable, but because there is a fairer chance of appetite and sleep after the exercise of laughing (be the laughter about anything or nothing) than after a day of uncomfortable listlessness.

A calm is a much less disagreeable affair—though it is not common to say so. A dead calm affords a fine opportunity to the gentlemen for writing and reading; and to the ladies, for the repairs of the wardrobe. Sewing, which I think a pleasant employment everywhere else, is trying to the head at sea; and many omissions and commissions may be observed in the matter of costume, which the parties would be ashamed of on land. The difference after a calm is remarkable: the cap-borders are spruce; the bonnets wear a new air; the gloves are whole: the married gentlemen appear with complete sets of buttons, and rectified stocks. The worst quality of a calm is that it tries tempers a little too far. If there be an infirmity of temper, it is sure to come out then. At such a time, there is much playing of shuffle-board upon deck; and the matches do not always end harmoniously. "You touched mine with your foot."—"I did not, I declare." "Now, don't say so, &c., &c."—"You

are eight."—"No, we are ten."—"I can show you you are only eight."—"Well, if you can't count any better than that,"—and so on. After three days of calm, there may be heard a subdued tone of scolding from the whist party at the top of the table, and a stray oath from some check-mated person lower down: and while the ladies are brushing their hair in their cabin, certain items of information are apt to be given of how Mr. A. looked when the lady's partner turned up trumps, and how shockingly Mr. B. pushed past Mr. C. in going up the cabin to dinner. The first breath of favourable wind, however, usually blows all these offences away, and tempers turn into their right course with the ship.

I had heard so much at home of the annoyances on board ship, that I made a list of them at the time for the consolation of my friends at home, who were, I suspected, bestowing more compassion upon me than I had any title to. I find them noted down as follows :—

Next to the sickness,—an annoyance scarcely to be exaggerated while it lasts, there is, first, the damp, clammy feel of everything you touch. Remedy, to wear gloves constantly, and clothes which are too bad to be spoiled. In this latter device, nearly the whole company were so accomplished, that it was hard to say who excelled.

Next, want of room. The remedy for this is a

tight, orderly putting away of everything; for which there is plenty of time.

Thirdly, the candles flare, and look untidy from running down twice as fast as they burn. Remedy, to go out of the way of them,—to the stern, for instance, where there are far better lights to be seen.

Fourthly, the seats and beds are all as hard as boards,—a grievance where one cannot always walk when one's limbs want resting with exercise. Remedy, patience. Perhaps air-cushions may be better still.

Fifthly, warning is given to be careful in the use of water. Remedy, to bathe in sea-water, and drink cider at dinner.

Sixthly, the cider is apt to get low. Remedy, take to soda water, ale, hock, or claret.

Seventhly, the scraping of the deck sets one's teeth on edge. For this I know of no remedy but patience; for the deck must be scraped.

Eighthly, the rattling, stamping, and clattering overhead, when the sails are shifted in the night. Remedy, to go to sleep again.

Ninthly, sour bread. Remedy, to eat biscuit instead.

Tenthly, getting sunburnt. Remedy, not to look in the glass.

These are all that I can allow from my own

experience. Some people talk of danger; but I do not believe there is more than in travelling on land. Some have called a ship a prison so often, that the saying seems to have become current. But, in my idea, the evils of a prison are, the being coerced by another person's will; the being disgraced; the being excluded from the face of nature; and the being debarred from society, employment, and exercise. None of these objections apply to a ship as a residence. As for the one point of resemblance, the being unable to walk a mile or more out and back again, of how many persons is this the voluntary choice, who were never either in a prison or a ship? I would never take the responsibility of recommending any elderly, or nervous, or untravelled persons to put themselves into a place which will not keep still, nor anything in it, for a month or six weeks, and from which they cannot get out: but I cannot think the confinement, by itself, anything to be much complained of.

A bad captain must be the worst of annoyances, to judge by contrast from the comfort we enjoyed under the government of an exceedingly good one. We had all great faith in Captain Holdrege as an excellent sailor; and we enjoyed daily and hourly proofs of his kindness of heart, and desire to make everybody about him happy. It was amazing with what patience he bore the teazings of some who were perpetually wanting to know things that he could not possibly tell them;—when we should be at New York, and so forth. The gentleman who unconsciously supplied the most merriment to the party, waylaid the captain one busy morning,—one of the first when there had been anything for the captain to do, and he was in such a bustle that nobody else dreamed of speaking to him.

"Captain," said the gentleman, "I want to speak to you."

"Another time, sir, if you please. I am in a hurry now."

"But, captain, I want to speak to you very much."

"Speak then, sir, and be quick, if you please."

"Captain, I am very glad you have a cow on board,—because of the milk."

"Hum," said the captain, and went on with his business.

One Sunday morning, when we were on "the Banks," this gentleman came to me with a doleful face, to tell me that he thought we should have been at New York to-day. I found that he had actually expected this up to the night before, because he had been told, previous to sailing, that we should probably spend our fourth Sunday at New York. It was proposed to tell him that we should probably be in the Pacific by the next morning, to see whether he would believe it: but I believe the experiment was not ventured upon. Some of the passengers, talking one day at dinner of percussion caps, asked him whether they were used in a regiment of which he had frequently spoken. He replied that he did not know, as he had not inquired much into the costume of the army.

By the 23rd of August we were only about 120 miles N.W. of the Azores. On the 1st of September, when our thoughts wandered homewards to the sportsmen all abroad in the stubble, to the readers of monthly periodicals in which we were interested, and to our families who were doubtless fancying us on the point of landing, we were not far from where we were a week ago. We had had beautiful weather, but every variety of westerly wind with it. The passengers began to flag. The novels were all read; the ladies' work was all done; and shuffle-board and chess will not do for ever. The captain began to send up an occasional whet of cherrybounce to the ladies before dinner. For my own part, I was finishing my writing, and finding my first leisure for books; and I found myself forgetting New York, and losing sight of all I expected to see beyond it, in the pleasures of the sea. We were now scarcely half way. The turning point of the voyage came the next day, in the shape of a storm.

Before I went on board, I had said that I should like to witness a storm as fierce as we could escape

from without fatal damage. Some passenger repeated this wish of mine (very common in persons
going to sea for the first time) in the hearing of the
mate, who told the sailors; who, accordingly, were
overheard saying one afternoon, that I had better
come on deck, and see what I should see. My
clerical friend took the hint, and called me hastily,
to observe the crew make ready for a squall. I ran
up, and perceived the black line advancing over the
water from the horizon,—the remarkable indication
of a coming squall. The sailors were running up
the shrouds to get the sails in. The second mate
was aloft, in the post of danger, his long hair
streaming in the wind, while with us below all was
calm. The sails were got in, just in time. The
captain did not come down to dinner. Orders were
given to " splice the main-brace ;" for the crew had
been handling the ropes since four in the morning.
I saw them come for their grog, and then wait for
what might happen next. By sunset the sky was
tremendous; the sea rising, the wind moaning and
whistling strangely. When I staggered to the stern,
to bid the sea good night, according to custom, the
waters were splendidly luminous. Floods of blue
fire were dashed abroad from our bows, and beyond,
the whole expanse sparkled as with diamonds.

All night the noises would have banished sleep,
if we could have lain quiet. There was a roar of

wind; the waves dashed against the sides of the
ship, as if they were bursting in: water poured into
our cabin, though the skylight was fastened down.
A heavy fall was now and then heard from the other
cabin;—some passenger heaved out of his berth.
After five hours, I could hold in no longer, and a
tremendous lurch tossed me out upon the floor,
where I alighted upon my thimble and scissors, the
ottoman I was working (and which I had felt confident was far enough off), my clothes, books, and the
empty water bottle.   All these things were lying in
a wet heap.   I traversed the ladies' cabin to explore,
holding by whatever was fastened to the floor.   The
only dry place in which I could lie down was under
the table; and standing was out of the question: so
I brought a blanket and pillow, lay down with a
firm hold of the leg of the table, and got an hour's
welcome sleep; by which time the storm was
enough to have wakened the dead.   The state of
our cabin was intolerable;—the crashing of glass,
the complaining voices of the sick ladies, the creak-
ing and straining of the ship; and, above all, the
want of air, while the winds were roaring over head.
I saw no necessity for bearing all this: so, sick as I
was, I put my clothes on, swathed myself in one
cloak, and carried up another, wherewith to lash
myself to something on deck.

   There, all was so glorious that I immediately

stumbled down again to implore the other ladies to come up and be refreshed: but no one would listen to me. They were too ill.—I got the captain's leave to fasten myself to the post of the binnacle, promising to give no trouble, and there I saw the whole of the never-to-be-forgotten scene.

We were lying in the trough of the sea, and the rolling was tremendous. The captain wished to wear round, and put out a sail, which, though quite new, was instantly split to ribands; so that we had to make ourselves contented where we were. The scene was perfectly unlike what I had imagined. The sea was no more like water than it was like land or sky. When I had heard of the ocean running mountains high, I thought it a mere hyperbolical expression. But here the scene was of huge wandering mountains,—wandering as if to find a resting-place,—with dreary leaden vales between. The sky seemed narrowed to a mere slip overhead, and a long-drawn extent of leaden waters seemed to measure a thousand miles ; and these were crested by most exquisite shades of blue and green where the foam was about to break. The heavens seemed rocking their masses of torn clouds, keeping time with the billows to the solemn music of the winds ; the most swelling and mournful music I ever listened to. The delight of the hour I shall not forget: it was the only new scene I had ever beheld that I had totally and unsuspectingly failed to imagine.

It was impossible to remain longer than noon, unless we meant to be drowned. When two or three gentlemen had been almost washed off, and the ship had been once nearly half her length under water, it was time to go below,—sad as the necessity was. The gale gradually abated. In the afternoon the ladies obtained leave to have their skylight opened, their cabin mopped, and the carpets taken up and carried away to dry.

The sailors got the mate to inquire how I liked the storm. If I was not satisfied now, I never should be. I was satisfied, and most thankful. The only thing that surprised me much was, that there was so little terrific about it. I was not aware till the next day, when the captain was found to have set it down a hurricane in the log-book, how serious a storm it was. The vessel is so obviously buoyant, that it appears impossible to overwhelm her; and we were a thousand miles from any rocks. In the excitement of such an hour, one feels that one would as soon go down in those magnificent waters as die any other death; but there was nothing present which impressed me with the idea of danger but the terrors of two of the passengers. Of the poor ladies I can give no account; but one gentleman pulled his travelling cap forward over his eyes, clasped his hands on his knees, and sat visibly shaking in a corner of the round-house, looking shrunk to half his size. The fears of another I regarded with more respect, because he tried hard to hide them. He followed me throughout, talking in an artist-like style about the tints, and the hues, and many other things that were to be noted, but not talked about at the moment. If he succeeded in covering up his fears from himself, one may well excuse the bad taste of the means employed. My clerical friend did better. He was on the watch for others and for himself. In high exhilaration, he helped every body, saw every thing, and will, to the end of his days, I will answer for it, forget nothing of that glorious time.

After the storm, we met with few delays. A calm of nine hours enabled the crew to repair all damage sustained; the rest of the time we were making progress, though it was sometimes very slow. We went south of " the Banks," and so missed something beside the fogs,—our hoped-for treat of fresh cod, and the spectacle of the fishermen's boats. Hereabouts the dog in the steerage smelt land, and stood snuffing, with his paws on the rail. A wild pigeon flew on board, too,—supposed to be from Newfoundland; and the air was sensibly colder, as it becomes on approaching the shore. The lottery with which the gentlemen had amused themselves became now very interesting. It consisted of ten tickets, at a sovereign each, answering to the ten days during which it had been thought probable that we should land. The two earliest were now sold for a shilling and eighteen-pence; and the captain gave £5 for the last, which bore date the 11th. This seemed to indicate the captain's expectation that our progress would still be slow; but we were scarcely more likely to land on the 11th than on the 4th or 5th.

A passenger beckoned the captain out of the cabin one evening, about this time, and asked him to look down into the hold, where a tallow candle, with a long wick, was seen leaning over the side of a candlestick, which was standing on a heap of loose cotton! Such are the perils that careless sailors will expose themselves and others to. The captain took care to impress his crew with his opinion on the matter.

I believe a regular piece of amusement on board these packet-ships is emptying the letter-bags out on the deck. A fine morning is chosen for this; and to a person who sits on the rail it affords a pretty picture. The ladies draw their chairs round the immense heap of letters; the gentlemen lie at length, and scarcely an epistle escapes comment. A shout of mirth bursts forth now and then, at some singular name, or mode of address; commonly at some Irish epistle, addressed to an emigrant in some out-of-the-way place, which there is scarcely room to insert, though the direction runs from corner to corner, over the whole square.

About this time, a pedlar, who was among the steerage passengers, appeared on deck, with his wares. His pretence was, that some of his silk handkerchiefs and gloves had got slightly spotted at sea, and that he was not so anxious as before to carry them to New York. However this might be, the merchant showed himself a shrewd man. He saw that the pleasure of shopping, after being for some weeks out of sight of land, would open to him the purse of many a passenger. It was most amusing to see the eagerness of both gentlemen and ladies, and their pleasure in purchases which they would have disdained on shore. For the next two or three days the company was spruce in damaged handkerchiefs and ribands, and mildewed gloves, rending in all directions; while the pedlar escaped duties, and stepped ashore with a heavy purse and light pack.

On the 15th, we were still between five and six hundred miles from our port. A sheep had jumped overboard, and so cheated us of some of our mutton. The vegetables were getting very dry. It was found best not to look into the dishes of dried fruits which formed our dessert. All was done that care

and cookery could do ; but who could have anticipated such a length of voyage ?　Open declarations
of *ennui* began to be made by not a few ; and I was
almost afraid to own, in answer to questions, that I
was not tired of the sea : but I could not honestly
say that I was.　The gentlemen began to spar at
table about the comparative merits of England and
America : the Prussian could not find English in
which to bemoan himself sufficiently, and shrugged.
The cider, ale, soda-water, and claret were all gone,
and we were taking to porter, which must needs
soon come to an end.　Some show of preparation
to land was this day made, and a lively bustle ensued
on the first hint from the captain.　He went round
to take down the names of the passengers at length,
in order to their being reported on arrival.　The
ages had to be affixed to the names ; and as the
captain could not ask the ladies for their ages, he
committed it to the gentlemen to decide upon each.
The ladies, who were quilling, trimming, and sorting
their things in their own cabin, could not conceive
the meaning of the shouts of laughter which came
from the top of the gentlemen's table, till the young
Carolinian came and told what the fun was.　The
standing joke is to make the young ladies many
years too old, and the old ladies ridiculously young :
and this was done now, the ladies considering the
affair no business of theirs.　One lady, who had

frequently crossed, told me that ten years before she had been set down as forty: she stood now as twenty-four.

On the 17th, we were surrounded with weed, and Mother Carey's chickens began to disappear. Soundings were this day taken, and I was called to see and touch the first American soil,—the thimble-full deposited on the lead. The next day, Thursday, the wind continuing fair, we were within 100 miles of our port, and all was liveliness and bustle.

The American divine was requested by all the passengers to propose, after dinner, the health of Captain and Mrs. Holdrege, using the opportunity to express our hearty thanks to the captain for the whole of his conduct towards us. The captain rose to speak in acknowledgment of the toast, but was so taken by surprise with his lady's name being hailed with our good wishes, that after two words of thanks, he shot out of the cabin, every one understanding the cause of his brevity. In the evening we were told that we should see land on rising in the morning; and some of us requested to be called at five.

At five, on the morning of the 19th, I started up, and at the foot of the companion-way was stopped by the Scotch lady, who told me I might go back again, as we were becalmed, and I might see the shore just as well two hours hence. This

was being a little too cool about such a matter. I
saw the dim shore,—a long line of the New Jersey
coast, with distinguishable trees and white houses.
By breakfast-time our eyes were painfully strained,
as only one could have the glass at a time, and I did
not like to snatch it from those who were enjoying
the pleasure of recognising familiar objects,—tracing
the first features of home. I was taken by surprise
by my own emotions. All that I had heard of the
Pilgrim Fathers, of the old colonial days, of the
great men of the Revolution, and of the busy,
prosperous succeeding days, stirred up my mind,
while I looked upon the sunny reach of land on the
horizon. All the morning I sat dreaming, interrupted now and then by the smiling but tearful
young mother, who expected tidings of her child
before the day was over; or by others, who had
less cause for being deeply moved, who came to
describe to me the pleasures of Long Branch, (the
bathing place in view,) or to speculate on how long
this tedious calm would last. All the morning I
sat on the rail, or played sister Anne to the ladies
below, when once the wind had freshened, and we
glided slowly along towards Sandy Hook. " Now
I see a large white house." " Now I see Neversink. Come up and see Neversink!" " Now I
see a flock of sheep on the side of a hill; and now
a fisherman standing beside his boat :" and so forth.

What were the ladies below for?—They were dressing for the shore. The gentlemen too vanished from the deck, one by one, and reappeared in glossy hats, coats with the creases of the portmanteau upon them, and the first really black shoes and boots we had seen for weeks. The quizzing which was properly due to the discarded sea garments was now bestowed on this spruce costume; and every gentleman had to encounter a laugh as he issued from the companion-way. We agreed to snatch our meals as we pleased this day. No one was to remain at table longer than he liked.—Everything looked joyous. The passengers were in the most amiable mood: we were in sight of a score of ships crossing the bar at Sandy Hook: the last company of porpoises was sporting alongside, and shoals of glittering white fish rippled the water. The captain was fidgetty, however. Those vessels crossing the bar might be rival packet-ships, and no pilot was yet to be seen. "Here he is!" cried a dozen voices at once; and an elegant little affair of a boat was seen approaching. A curious-looking old gentleman swung himself up, and seemed likely to be torn in pieces by the ravenous inquirers for news. He thrust an armful of newspapers among us, and beckoned the captain to the stern, where the two remained in grave consultation for a few minutes, when the captain called one of the lady passengers aside, to ask her a question.   What the pilot wanted to know was, whether George Thompson, the Abolition missionary, was on board.   He was to have been, but was not.   The pilot declared that this was well, as he could not have been landed without the certainty of being destroyed within a week—the Abolition riots in New York having taken place just before.   What the captain wanted to learn of the lady passenger was, what my opinions on slavery were, in order to know whether he might safely land me.   She told him that I was an abolitionist in principle ; but that she believed I went to America to learn and not to teach.   So the good captain nodded, and said nothing to me on the subject.

Next arrived a boat from the newspaper office of the Courier and Inquirer, whose agent would not hear of dinner, or any other delay, but shouldered his bag of news, got the list of our names, and was off.—The American passengers, all by this time good friends of mine, came to show me, with much mirth, paragraphs in the newspapers the pilot had brought, exhorting their readers not to chew tobacco or praise themselves in my presence, under penalty of being reported of in London for these national foibles.

After dinner, we were off Sandy Hook, and the hills of New Jersey, Long Island, and Staten Island were growing purple in the cloudy sunset, when a small, shabby steam-boat was seen emerging from the Narrows. O, the speculations and breathless suspense as to whether she was coming to us! In a few minutes, there remained no further doubt. Then there was a rush to the side, and one of the young ladies saw through her tears her two brothers, and other passengers other relations showing themselves on the bows of the steamer. They presently boarded us, we strangers having all retired to the other side. I never liked introductions better than those which followed. With broad smiles my passenger friends came up, saying, " I have the great pleasure of introducing to you my brother."—" I am sure you will be glad to hear that my family are all well." These are occasions when sympathy is very sweet, and when it is always ready.

Then was heard the captain's loudest voice, crying, " All who wish to go up to the city to-night, get ready directly." We had all previously agreed how much better it was that we should spend this night on board, as the harbour would be seen to much advantage by the morning light: but we forgot all this in a moment, and nobody dreamed of being left behind. Our little bundles were made

up in a trice, and we quitted our ship. The crew
and steerage passengers assembled on deck, and
gave us three parting cheers, which might be heard
all over the harbour. Our gentlemen returned
them, and our hearts yearned towards our beautiful
ship, as she sat dark upon the evening waters, with
all her sails majestically spread. " Does she not
look well now?" " Does she not show herself beautifully now?" exclaimed one and another, in the
hearing of the gratified captain.

The light was failing as we entered the Narrows.
The captain and several other friends pointed out
to me every headland, bay, and fortification as we
passed.—We were detained a long while at the
quarantine ground. The doctor was three miles
off, and nearly an hour elapsed before the great
news reached him that we were all quite well, and
we were therefore allowed to proceed. It now
rained heavily, and we were obliged to crowd into
the small cabin of the poorest steamer in the bay.
There, by the light of one dim and dirty lamp, was
the question first asked me in joke, which has since
been repeated in so many moods, " How do you
like America?" The weather cleared up in another
half hour. We stood in the dark on the wet deck,
watching the yellow lights and shadowy buildings of
the shore we were rapidly nearing, till we felt the

expected shock, and jumped upon the wharf amidst the warm welcomes of many friends, who, in their own joy at alighting on their native shore, did not forget to make it at once a home to us strangers.

This was at eight in the evening of the 19th of September, 1834, after a long but agreeable voyage of forty-two days.

FIRST IMPRESSIONS.

" Navigia, atque agri culturas, mœnia, leges
  Arma, vias, vesteis, et cætera de genere horum
  Præmia, delicias quoque vitæ funditus omneis,
  Carmina, picturas, ac dædala signa, politus
  Usus, et impigræ simul experientia mentis,
  Paullatim docuit pedetentim progredienteis."
                                    Lucretius, lib. v.

THE moment of first landing in a foreign city is
commonly spoken of as a perfect realization of
forlornness. My entrance upon American life was
anything but this. The spirits of my companions
and myself were in a holiday dance while we were
receiving our first impressions; and New York
always afterwards bore an air of gaiety to me from
the association of the early pleasures of foreign
travel.

Apartments had been secured for us at a boarding-house in Broadway, and a hackney-coach was
in waiting at the wharf. The moonlight was flick-
ering through the trees of the battery, the insects
were buzzing all about us, the catydids were grind-
ing, and all the sounds, except human voices, were
quite unlike all we had heard for six weeks. One
of my companions took the sound of the catydid
for a noise in her head, for many hours after coming
into their neighbourhood. As we rattled over the

stones, I was surprised to find that the street we were in was Broadway;—the lower and narrower end, however: but nothing that I saw, after all I had heard, and the panorama of New York that I had visited in London, disappointed me so much as Broadway. Its length is remarkable; but neither its width, nor the style of its houses. The trees with which it is lined gave it, this first evening, a foreign air.

Our hostess at the boarding-house shook hands with us, and ordered tea. While we waited for it, and within ten minutes after I had crossed the first American threshold, three gentlemen introduced themselves to me, one of whom was the melancholy politician, whom I have mentioned elsewhere* as having forewarned me of the total overthrow of the United States' institutions, which would certainly take place while I was in the country. This gentleman afterwards became a dear and intimate friend; and we found that politics are, perhaps, the only subject on which we entertain irreconcileable differences of opinion. We often amused ourselves with recurring to this our first meeting. This gentleman afforded me an early specimen of the humour which I think one of the chief characteristics of the Americans. In the few minutes during which we were waiting for tea, he dropped

* Society in America, vol. i., p. 10.

some drolleries so new to me, and so intense, that I was perplexed what to do with my laughter.

While we were at tea, a few gentlemen dropped in, and read the newspapers at the long table at which we were seated. One fixed my attention at once. He had the carriage of a soldier, with an uncommonly fine countenance, bearing a general resemblance to the great men of the Revolution with whose portraits the English are most familiar. I think it is not a mere fancy that there is an air common to Washington, Jefferson, and Madison. This gentleman reminded me of them all; and the quietness with which he made his remarks, and his evident high breeding, piqued the curiosity of a stranger. He was General Mason, the father of the young Governor of Michigan, and the most eminent citizen of Detroit. From time to time in my travels, I met various members of his family, whose kindness always made me thankful that accident had placed me in the same house with them at the outset.

In our rooms, we found beds with four posts, looking as if meant to hang gowns and bonnets upon; for there was no tester. The washstand was without tumbler, glass, soap, or brush-tray. The candlestick had no snuffers. There was, however, the luxury, sufficient for the occasion, that every article of furniture stood still in its place; and that the apartment itself did not rock up and down. The first few days after a voyage go far towards making one believe that some things have a quality of stability, however one may be metaphysically convinced that the sea affords a far truer hint of the incessant flux and change which are the law of the universe. If I had rejoiced in the emblem at sea, I now enjoyed the deception on land.

At five in the morning I threw up my sash, to see what I could see. I cannot conceive what travellers mean by saying that there is little that is foreign in the aspect of New York. I beheld nothing at this moment that I could have seen at home, except the sky and the grass of the court-yard. The houses were all neatly and brightly painted, had green outside blinds to every window, and an apparatus for drying linen on the roof. A young lady in black silk, with her hair neatly dressed, was mopping the steps of one house; and a similar young lady was dusting the parlour of another. A large locust-tree grew in the middle of the court-yard of the house I was in; and under it was a truly American wood-pile. Two negroes were at the pump, and a third was carrying musk-melons.

When the breakfast-bell rang, the long and cross tables in the eating-room were filled in five minutes. The cross table, at which our hostess presided, was occupied by General Mason's family, a party of

Spaniards, and ourselves. The long one was filled up with families returning southwards from the Springs; married persons without children, who preferred boarding to housekeeping; and single gentlemen, chiefly merchants. I found this mode of living rather formidable the first day; and not all the good manners that I witnessed at public tables ever reconciled me to it.

From a trunk belonging to a lady of our party having been put on board a wrong ship, we had some immediate shopping to do, and to find a mantua-maker. We suspected we should soon be detained at home by callers, and therefore determined to transact our business at once, though our luggage had not arrived from the Custom-House, and we were not " dressed for Broadway," as the phrase is.

In the streets, I was in danger of being run down by the fire-engines, so busy were my eyes with the novelties about me. These fire-engines run along the side-pavement, stopping for nobody; and I scarcely ever walked out in New York without seeing one or more out on business, or for an airing. The novelties which amused me were the spruce appearance of all the people; the pervading neatness and brightness, and the business-like air of the children. The carmen were all well dressed, and even two poor boys who were selling matches had clean shirt-collars and whole coats, though they were barefooted. The stocks of goods seemed large and handsome, and we were less struck with the indifference of manner, commonly ascribed to American storekeepers, than frequently afterwards. The most unpleasant circumstance was the appearance and manner of the ladies whom we saw in the streets and stores. It was now the end of a very hot summer, and every lady we met looked as if she were emerging from the yellow fever; and the languid unsteady step betokened the reverse of health.

The heat was somewhat oppressive. We were in the warm dresses we had put on while yet at sea, as our trunks had not made their appearance. Trains of callers came in the afternoon and evening; members of Congress, candidates for State offices, fellow-passengers and their friends, and other friends of our friends; and still we were not " dressed for Broadway." In the evening, the luggage of my companions was brought up, but not mine. Special orders had been issued from the Custom-House that my baggage should pass without examination; and it was therefore at this moment on board ship. To-night it was too late : next morning it was Sunday, and everything in the hold was under lock and key, and unattainable till Monday. There seemed no hope of my getting out all day, and I was really vexed. I wanted to see the churches, and hear the preaching, and be doing what others were doing;

but the heat was plainly too great to be encountered in any gown but a muslin one. A lady boarding in the house happened to hear of the case, and sent her servant to say that she believed her dresses would fit me, and that she should be happy to supply me with a gown and bonnet till my trunks should arrive. I accepted her kind offer without any scruple, feeling that a service like this was just what I should wish to render to any lady under the same circumstances: so I went to church equipped in a morning-gown and second-best bonnet of this neighbourly lady's.

The church that we went to was the Unitarian church in Chambers street. Its regular pastor was absent, and a professional brother from Philadelphia preached. We were most deeply impressed by the devotional part of his service, delivered in a voice which I have certainly never heard equalled for music and volume. His discourse moved us no less. We looked at one another in much delight. I warned my companion not to be too certain that this preaching was all we then felt it to be: we had been six Sundays at sea, and some of the impression might be owing to this being the renewal of the privilege of social worship in a church. I heard much of the same preaching afterwards, however; and I am now of the same opinion that I was this first day,—that it is the most true, simple, and solemn that I ever listened to. The moment the service was over, the minister came down from the pulpit, addressed me as an old friend, and requested me to accept the hospitality of his house when I should visit Philadelphia. Under the emotions of the hour, it was impossible to help giving a glad assent : and in his house I afterwards enjoyed many weeks of an intercourse as intimate as can ever exist between members of the same family. We kept up the most rapid and copious correspondence the whole time I was in America, and he and his wife were my American brother and sister,—the depositories of all those "impressions" on the mind of a stranger about which American society is so anxious.

General Mason introduced me to Governor Cass, then Secretary-at-War ; now Ambassador at Paris. Governor Cass is a shrewd, hard-looking man, the very concentration of American caution. He is an accomplished and an honest man ; but his dread of committing himself renders both his solid and ornamental good qualities of less value to society than they should be. The State of Michigan, which is under great obligations to him, is proud of her citizen ; and it is agreed, I believe, on all hands, that his appointment is more satisfactory and honourable to his country than that of many who have been sent as ministers to foreign courts.

I feel some doubt about giving any account of the

public men of the United States; I do not mean
scruples of conscience; for when a man comes forward in political, or other kind of public life, he
makes a present of himself to society at large, and
his person, mind, and manners become a legitimate
subject of observation and remark.   My doubts arise
from the want of interest in the English about the
great men of America; a want of interest which
arises from no fault in either party, I believe; but
from the baseness of the newspapers, whose revilings
of all persons in turn who fill a public station are
so disgusting as to discourage curiosity, and set all
friendly interest at defiance.   The names of the
English political leaders of the day are almost as
familiar in the mouths of Americans as of natives,
while people in London are asking who Mr. Clay
is, and what part of the Union Mr. Calhoun comes
from.   The deeds of Mr. Clay, and the aspirations
of Mr. Calhoun would be at least as interesting in
London as the proceedings of French and German
statesmen, if they could be fairly placed under observation : but every man of feeling and taste recoils
from wading through such a slough of rancour, folly
and falsehood as the American newspapers present
as the only medium through which the object is to
be attained.

Mr. Gallatin's name is, however, everywhere
known and welcome.   Mr. Gallatin did me the

honour of calling on me in New York, having heard
that I desired to learn the precise grounds of the
quarrel which was agitating the country about the
Bank. I was delighted to listen to his full and luminous report of the question; and of many other
matters, on which he spoke with a freedom and
courtesy which would go far towards making the
current of human affairs run smooth, if they were
but general. He told me something of the early
part of his career, which began in 1787; described
his three visits to England, and sketched the character of the reigns of our two last kings, of Louis
Philippe, and of President Jackson. He entered
upon the philosophy of the Presidentship; exhibited
the spirit of the three great divisions of the United
States, the north, south, and west; explained the
principles on which the letting of land proceeds;
described the Germans and other agricultural population of the country, and showed the process by
which the aristocratic class rises and is replenished
in a democratic republic. While he was talking, I
felt as if he was furnishing me with new powers of
observation; and when he was gone, I hastened to
secure what he had told me, lest its novelty and
abundance should deceive my memory. I believe
Mr. Gallatin was at this time seventy-two: but he
did not appear so old. He is tall, and looks dig
nified and courteous. He is a native of Switzerland,

and speaks with a very slight foreign accent, but with a flow and liveliness which are delightful.

I was assured, at the outset, that the late abolition riots in New York were the work of the Irish immigrants, who feared the increase of a free black population, as likely to interfere with their monopoly of certain kinds of labour. This I afterwards found to be untrue. Some Irish may have joined in "the row," but the mischief originated with natives. It is remarkable that I heard no more of abolition for many weeks; I think not till I was about leaving Philadelphia.

We obtained some "impressions" of the environs of New York, to add to those we had of the city itself, by going to spend an evening at Mr. King's, at High Wood, two miles beyond Hoboken, on the New Jersey side of the river. The frame cottages, with their thatched verandahs, struck me as very pretty. I could not say much for the beauty of the corn, whose plants, long since stripped of their cobs, were standing yellow and dry, and fast hastening to decay. There were ridges of grey rock, interspersed with woods which still flourished in their summer greenness. Above all, was a sunset which, if seen in England, would persuade the nation that the end of the world was come. The whole arch of the sky appeared lined with conflagration. It seemed strange to see the wagon-driver talking with his bullocks, and the old Dutch dame spinning in the stoup, as quietly as if that scarlet sky had been of its usual summer blue.

I was shown, on the way, the spot where Hamilton received his death wound from Colonel Burr. It was once made a qualification for office that the candidate should never have fought a duel. Duelling is an institution not to be reached by such a provision as this. No man under provocation to fight would refrain from fear of disqualifying himself for office hereafter; and the operation of the restriction was accordingly found to be this; that duels were as frequent as ever, and that desirable candidates were excluded. The provision was got rid of on the plea that promissory oaths are bad in principle. The cure of duelling, as of every other encroachment of passion and selfishness on such higher principles as, being passive, cannot be embodied in acts, must be the natural result of the improved moral condition of the individual or of society. No one believes that the legal penalties of duelling have had much effect in stopping the practice; and it is an injury to society to choose, out of the ample range of penalties, disqualification for social duty as one.

The view from Mr. King's garden at High Wood is beautiful. From one opening, a reach of twelve miles of the Hudson is commanded,—from

the Narrows upwards.   A soft red light was resting on the waters, the last tinge from the late
flaming sky.   The dark sloops moored below were
thus rendered visible, while the twilight shrouded
the rocks.   Opposite, there was a flare in the woods,
from a glass-house; and the lights of the city
twinkled afar off, reflected in the waters.

One of the first impressions of a foreigner in
New York is of the extreme insolence and vulgarity
of certain young Englishmen, who thus make themselves very conspicuous.   Well-mannered Englishmen are scarcely distinguishable from the natives,
and thus escape observation; while every commercial traveller who sneers at republicanism all day
long, and every impertinent boy, leaving home for
the first time, with no understanding or sympathy
for anything but what he has been accustomed to
see at home, obtrudes himself upon the notice, and
challenges the congeniality of such countrymen and
countrywomen as he can contrive to put himself in
the way of.   I was annoyed this evening, on my
return home, by a very complete specimen of the
last-mentioned order of travellers.

Need I say, after thus detailing the little incidents which followed my landing in America, that
my first impressions of the country were highly
agreeable?

THE HUDSON.

" O, there is not lost
One of earth's charms : upon her bosom yet,
After the flight of untold centuries,
The freshness of her far beginning lies,
And yet shall lie."

Bryant.

I went three times up the Hudson; and if I lived
at New York, should be tempted to ascend it three
times a-week during the summer. Yet the greater
number of ladies on board the steam-boat remained
in the close cabin, among the crying babies, even
while we were passing the finest scenery of the
river. They do not share the taste of a gentleman who, when I was there, actually made the
steam-boat his place of abode during the entire
summer season, sleeping on board at Albany and
New York on alternate nights, and gazing at the
shores all the day long, with apparently undiminish-
ing delight.

The first time we went up, the early part of the
morning was foggy, and the mist hung about the
ridge of the Palisades,—the rocky western barrier
of the river. There were cottages perched here
and there, and trees were sprinkled in the crevices;

and a little yellow strand, just wide enough for the fisherman and his boat, now and then intervened between the waters and the perpendicular rock. In the shadowy recesses of the shore were sloops moored. Seagulls dipped their wings in the gleams of the river, and the solitary fish-hawk sailed slowly over the woods. I saw on the eastern bank, a wide flight of steps cut in the turf, leading to an opening in the trees, at the end of which stood a white house, apparently in deep retirement.—Further on, the river widened into the Tappaan sea, and then the hills rose higher behind the banks, and wandering gleams lighted up a mountain region here and there. The captain admitted us, as strangers, (of course without any hint from us) into the wheel-room, which was shady, breezy, roomy, and commanding the entire view. Hence we were shown Mr. Irving's cottage, the spot where André was captured, and the other interesting points of the scenery. Then the banks seemed to close, and it was matter for conjecture where the outlet was. The waters were hemmed in by abrupt and dark mountains, but the channel was still broad and smooth enough for all the steam-boats in the republic to ride in safety. Ridges of rock plunged into the waters, garnished with trees which seemed to grow without soil : above them were patches of cultivation on the mountain sides, and slopes of cleared land, with white houses

upon them. Doves flitted among the nearest trees,
and gay row-boats darted from point to point, from
one island to another.

West Point, beautiful as it is, was always visible
too soon. Yet to leave the boat was the only way to
remain in sight of the Highlands ; and the charms of
the place itself are scarcely to be surpassed.—The
hotel is always full of good company in the season.
Mr. Cozens keeps a table for the officers, and is
permitted to add as many guests as his house will
hold : but, under such circumstances, he takes pains
to admit only such as are fit company for his per-
manent boarders. The views from the hotel are so
fine, and there is such a provision of comfort and
entertainment, that there would be no hardship in
sitting within doors for a week : but we made the
best use we could of our opportunities, and saw and
achieved everything pertaining to the place, except
mounting the Crow's Nest; an expedition which the
heat of the weather prevented our undertaking.

In some solitary spots of this settlement the
stranger cannot help meditating on the vast materials of human happiness which are placed at the
disposal of the real administrators of this great
country. How great is the apparatus to be yet put
to use ! Here, where life is swarming all around,
how few are the habitations of men ! Here are
woods climbing above woods, to the clouds and

stretching to the horizon, in which myriads of creatures are chirping, humming, and sporting; clefts
whence the waters gush out; green slopes ready for
the plough and the sickle; flat meadows with a few
haycocks lying at the foot of mountains as yet un-
touched. Grasshoppers spring at every step one
takes in the rich grass, and many a blue dragon-fly
balances itself on the tips of the strongest blades;
butterflies, green, black, white, and yellow, dazzle
the eye that would follow them; yet how few men
are near ! A gay group on the steps of the hotel,
a company of cadets parading on the green; the
ferryman and his fare, and the owners of this and
that and the other house perched upon the pinnacles
of the hills;—these are all as yet visible in a region
which will hereafter be filled with speech and busy
with thought.

On the steep above the landing-place I was
introduced to Mr. Irving, with whom I had a few
minutes' conversation before he stepped into the
ferry-boat which was to take him over to the Foundry
to dinner. Many other persons with whom I was
glad to have the opportunity of becoming acquainted were at the hotel. Mr. and Mrs. Morris
were our guides to Fort Putnam, after dinner;
walkers as active and resolute as ourselves. The
beauty from this elevated platform is really oppressive to the sense. One is glad to divert one's

attention from its awful radiance by walking in
precipitous places, by visiting the cell in which it is
said, but doubtfully, that André was confined, or
even by meditating on the lot of the solitary cow
that has the honour of grazing in the midst of the
only ruins that adorn American scenery.

A lady in the hotel offered to meet me on the
house-top at five o'clock in the morning to see the
sun rise. I looked out at three; there was a solitary light twinkling in the academy, and a faint
gleam, out of a cloudy sky, upon the river. At
five the sky was so thickly overspread with clouds,
that the expedition to the house-top had to be aban-
doned. The morning afterwards cleared, and I
went alone down to Kosciusko's Garden. I loved
this retreat at an hour when I was likely to have it
to myself. It is a nook, scooped, as it were, out of
the rocky bank of the river, and reached by descending several flights of steps from the platform behind
the hotel and academy. Besides the piled rocks
and the vegetation with which they are clothed,
there is nothing but a clear spring, which wells up
in a stone basin, inscribed with the hero's name.
This was his favourite retreat; and here he sat for
many hours in a day, with his book and his thoughts.
After fancying for some time that I was alone, and
playing with the fountain and the leaves of the red
beech and the maple, now turning into its autumnal

scarlet, I found, on looking up, that one of the cadets was stretched at length on a high projection of rock, and that another was coming down the steps. The latter accosted me, offering to point out to me the objects of interest about the place. We had a long conversation about his academical life.

The students apply themselves to mathematics during the first and second years; during the third, to mathematics, chemistry, and natural philosophy; and during the fourth, to engineering. There is less literary pursuit than they or their friends would like; but they have not time for everything. Their work is from seven in the morning till four in the afternoon, with the exception of two hours for meals. Then come drill and recreation, and then the evening parade. During six weeks (I think) of the summer, they camp out, which some of the youths enjoy, while others like it so much less than living under a roof, that they take this time to be absent on furlough. The friends of others come to see them, while the pretty spectacle of a camp is added to the attractions of the place. Every care is used that the proficiency should be maintained at the highest point that it can be made to reach. The classes consist of not less than 140, of whom only 40 graduate. Some find the work too hard; some dislike the routine; others are postponed; and by this careful weeding out, the choicest are kept for

the public service. This process may go some
way towards accounting for the present unpopularity
of the institution, and the consequent danger of its
downfal. The number of disappointed youths,
whose connexions will naturally bear a grudge
against the establishment, must be great. There
is a belief abroad that its principle and administration are both anti-republican; and in answer to an
irresistible popular demand, a committee of Congress has been engaged in investigating both the
philosophy and practice of this national military
academy; for some time previous to which there
was difficulty in obtaining the annual appropriation
for its support. I have not seen the Report of this
Committee, but I was told that the evidence on
which it is founded is very unfavourable to the
conduct of the establishment, in a political point of
view. The advantages of such an institution in
securing a uniformity of military conduct in case
of war, from the young soldiers of all the States
having received a common education; in affording
one meeting point where sectional prejudice may
be dissolved; and in concentrating the attention of
the whole union upon maintaining a high degree of
proficiency in science, are so great, that it is no
wonder that an indignant and honest cry is raised
against those who would abolish it on account of its
aristocratic tendencies. I rather think it is a case

in which both parties are more than commonly right: that it is an institution which can scarcely be dispensed with, but which requires to be watched with the closest jealousy, that there may be no abuse of patronage, and no such combination as could lead to the foundation of a military aristocracy.

I saw the well-selected library, consisting of several thousand volumes, the spacious lecture rooms, and students' apartments. I often wonder whether students are at all aware of the wistful longing,—the envy—with which those who are precluded from academical life, view the arrangements of colleges. No library in a private house conveys any idea of the power of devotion to study which is suggested by the sight of a student's apartment in a college. The sight of the snug solitary room, the bookshelves, the single desk and arm-chair, the larum, and even the flower-pot or two in the window, and the portrait of some favorite philosophical worthy,—these things send a thrill of envy through the heart of the thoughtful politician, or man of business, or woman, who cannot command such facilities for study. I know that the fallacy of attributing too much to external arrangements enters here: that many study to as much advantage under difficulties as any academical member in his retirement: —I know too that the student shares the human weakness of finding evil in his lot, and supposing

that he should be better in some other circumstances;—I know this by a revelation once made to
me by a college student, for whose facilities I had
been intensely thankful,—a revelation of his deep
and incessant trouble because he was living to himself, selfishly studying, and obliged to wait four or
five years before he could bestir himself for his
race;—yet, in spite of all this knowledge that the
common equality of pleasures and pains subsists
here, I never see the interior of a college without
longing to impress upon its inmates how envied and
enviable they are. It is difficult to remember that
the stillness of the cell is of no avail without the
intentness of the mind, and that there is no effica-
cious solitude in the deepest retirement, if the spirit
is roving abroad after schemes of pleasure or ambition,—or even of piety and benevolence, which are
not the appointed duty of the time. But I have
wandered from my new acquaintance in Kosciusko's
garden.

I was surprised to learn the extraordinary high
average of health the place can boast of. The
young men enter at the age of from fourteen to
twenty, stay three or four years, and number about
300 at a time. The mortality in the seventeen
years preceding my visit was only five. For eight
years before the winter of 1834, there had been no

death. Within a few months after, the superin-
tendent's wife, a servant, and a cadet died; and this
was, of course, considered an extraordinary mortality. I rather wondered at this account, for the
young men look anything but robust, and the use of
tobacco among them is very free indeed. It is
prohibited, but not the less indulged in on that
account,—nor from the absence of evil example in
their superintendents. My new acquaintance made
very frank confessions on this subject. He told me
that he believed the free use of tobacco had extensively and irreparably injured his health, and that
he bitterly mourned his first indulgence in it.

" Do not you mean to leave it off? " said I.

" No."

" Do you think you could not? "

" I could; but it would take three weeks to cure
myself; and during that time I could do nothing;
and I cannot afford that. I could not learn my
lessons without it, and the loss of three weeks would
injure all my prospects in life."

" Hardly so fatally as the ruin of your health, I
should think. Is your case a common one here?"

" Too common. But I assure you I do all I can
to prevent the bad consequences of my own example.
I warn my juniors as they come in, very seriously."

" Do you find your warnings of much use?"

" I am afraid not much."

" They have the usual fate of mere precept, I suppose ?"

" Yes, I am afraid so."

The manners of the cadets are excellent. They are allowed, under restrictions, to mix with the company at Mr. Cozens', and thus to be frequently in ladies' society. There is a book kept at the hotel, where every cadet must, at each visit, enter his name at length, and the duration of his stay.

The second time I was at West Point was during the camping-out season. The artillery drill in the morning was very noisy and grand to ladies who had never seen anything of the "pomp and circumstance of glorious war." Then the cadets retired to their tents; and the ladies flitted about all the morning, making calls on each other. When we had discharged this first of a traveller's duties, we sauntered to the cemetery. Never did I see such a spot to be buried in. The green hill projects into the river so that the monumental pillar erected by the cadets to the comrade who was killed by the bursting of a gun in 1817 is visible from two long reaches. One other accident had occurred a little while before : a cadet had been killed by a comrade in fencing. The tombs are few, and the inscriptions simple. Broad, spreading trees overshadow the long grass, and the whole is so hemmed in, so intensely quiet,

that no sound is to be heard but the plash of oars
from below, and the hum of insects around, except
when the evening gun booms over the heights, or the
summer storm reverberates among the mountains.

Such a storm I had witnessed the evening before
from the piazza of the hotel.   I stayed from the
parade to watch it.   As the thick veil of rain came
down, the mountains seemed to retire, growing
larger as they receded.   As the darkness advanced,
the scene became strangely compound.   A friend
sat with me in the piazza, talking of the deepest
subjects on which human thought can speculate.
Behind us were the open windows of the hotel,
where, by turning the head, we might see the
dancing going on,—the gallant cadets and their
pretty partners, while all the black servants of the
house ranged their laughing faces in the rear.   The
music of the ball-room came to us mingling with
the prolonged bursts of thunder : and other, and
grander strains rose from the river, where two large
steam-boats, with their lights, moved like constel-
lations on the water, conveying a regiment from
Pennsylvania which was visiting the soldiery of
New York State.   They sent up rockets into the
murky sky, and poured new blasts of music from
their band as they passed our promontory.   Every
moment the lightning burst ; now illuminating the
interior of a mass of clouds ; now quivering from

end to end of heaven; now shedding broad livid
gleams which suddenly revealed a solitary figure on
the terrace, a sloop on the waters, and every jutting
point of rock. Still the dance went on till the
hour struck which abruptly called the youths away
from their partners, and bade them hie to their tents.

On returning from the cemetery, we found Mr.
and Mrs. Kemble, from the opposite side of the
river, waiting to offer us their hospitality; and we
agreed to visit them in the afternoon. Mr. Kemble's
boat awaited us at the landing-place by three o'clock,
and we rowed about some time before landing on
the opposite bank, so irresistible is the temptation
to linger in this scene of magical beauty. The
catholic chapel of Coldspring is well placed on a
point above the river; and the village, hidden from
West Point by a headland, is pretty. From Mr.
Kemble's we were to be treated with a visit to the
Indian Fall, and were carried within half a mile
of it by water. We followed the brawling brook
for that distance, when we saw the glistening of
the column of water through the trees. No fall
can be prettier for its size, which is just small
enough to tempt one to climb. A gentleman of our
party made the attempt; but the rocks were too
slippery with wet weed, and he narrowly escaped
a tumble of twenty feet into the dark pool below.
The boys, after bringing us branches of the black

cherry, clustered with the fruit, found a safe and
dry way up, and appeared waving their green boughs
in triumph at the top of the rocks. The tide had
risen so that the river was brimming full as we
returned, and soft with the mountain shadows : but
we landed at West Point in time to see the sun
set,—twice, as it happened. At the landing-place
we stood to see it drop behind the mountain; but
just after we had bidden it good night, I saw that
a meditative cadet, lying at length upon a rock, was
still basking in the golden light, and I ran up the
steep to the piazza. There, in a gap between two
summits, was the broad disk, as round as ever ; and
once more we saw it sink in a tranquillity almost as
grand as the stormy splendour of the preceding
night.—Then ensued the evening parade; guitar
music in the hotel : and dancing in the camp.

This evening, a lady and her daughter steamed
down from Fishkill with a request to us to spend a
few days there ; and a clergyman steamed up from
New York with an invitation from Dr. Hosack to
visit him and his family at Hyde Park. We could
not do both ; and there was some difficulty in contriving to do either, anxiously as we desired it ;
but we presently settled that Fishkill must be given
up, and that we must content ourselves with two
days at Hyde Park.

The next morning, I experienced a sensation

which I had often heard of, but never quite believed in;—the certainty that one has wakened in another world.—Those who have travelled much, know that a frequent puzzle, on waking from sound sleep in new places, is to know where one is,—even in what country of the world. This night, I left my window open, close to my head, so that I could see the stars reflected in the river. When I woke, the scene was steeped in the light of the sunrise, and as still as death. Its ineffable beauty was all; I remarked no individual objects; but my heart stood still with an emotion which I should be glad to think I may feel again, whenever I really do enter a new scene of existence. It was some time before my senses were separately roused; during the whole day, I could not get rid of the impression that I had seen a vision; and even now I can scarcely look back upon the scene as the very same which at other hours I saw clouded with earth-drawn vapours, and gilded by the common sun.

At eleven o'clock, we left West Point; and I am glad that we felt sure at the time that we should visit it again;—a design which we did not accomplish, as the place was ravaged by scarlet fever at the season of the next year that we had fixed for our visit.—Mr. Livingston, who had just returned from his French mission, was on board the boat. My letters of introduction to him were at the bottom of my trunk ; but we did not put off becoming acquainted till I could get at them.

Mr. Livingston's name is celebrated and honoured in England, (as over all Europe) through its connexion with the Louisiana Code,—this gentleman's great work. He was born and educated in the State of New York. While pursuing his studies at Princeton College in 1779 and 1780, he was subject to strange interruptions ; 'the professors being repeatedly driven from their chairs by incursions of the enemy, and their scholars on such occasions forming a corps to go out and fight. The library was scattered, the philosophical apparatus destroyed, and the college buildings shared with troops quartered in the establishment : yet young Livingston quitted college a good scholar. He was a member of the fourth Congress, and there made himself remarkable by his exertions to ameliorate the criminal code of the United States, then as sanguinary as those of the Old World. In 1801, he returned to the practice of his profession of the law in New York, but was not long permitted to decline public life. He was appointed attorney of the state of New York, and mayor of the city. He remained in the city, in the discharge of his duties, while the yellow fever drove away every one who could remove. He nearly died of the disease, and was ruined in his private affairs by his devotion to the public service. In 1804, he resigned his offices, and retired to Louisiana, (then a new acquisition of the United States,) to retrieve his fortunes: and from thence he discharged all his obligations, paying his debts, with interest upon them, to the last farthing. He was deprived, by a mistake of President Jefferson's, of an immense property which he had acquired there, and was involved in expensive litigation of many years' duration. The law decided in his favour, and the controversy ended in a manner the most honourable to both parties; in a reciprocation of hearty good will.

During the invasion of Louisiana by the British, Mr. Livingston took a prominent part in the defence of the State: and when it was over, undertook, with two coadjutors, the formidable task of simplifying its laws, entangled as they were with Spanish prolixities, and all manner of unnecessary and unintelligible provisions. His system was adopted, and has been in use ever since. In 1820, the system of municipal law was revised at New Orleans, under the superintendence of Mr. Livingston, and his amendments were put in practice in 1823. He was at the same time engaged, without assistance, in preparing his celebrated penal code. When it was all ready for the press, in 1824, he sat up late one night, to ascertain finally the correctness of the fair copy; and, having finished, retired to rest, in a

state of calm satisfaction at his great work being
completed. He was awakened by a cry of fire.
The room where he had been employed was burning, and every scrap of his papers was consumed.
Not a note or memorandum was saved.

He appeared to be stunned for the hour; but
before the day closed he had begun his labours
again; and he never relaxed, till, in two years from
the time of the fire, he presented his work to the
legislature of Louisiana, improved by the reconsid-
eration which he had been compelled to give it.
Men of all countries who understand jurisprudence,
seem to think that no praise of this achievement can
be excessive.

He afterwards represented Louisiana in both
Houses of Congress, became Secretary of State in
1831 : and in 1833, Minister to France. His was
a busy life, of doing, suffering, and, we may confi-
dently add, enjoying : for his was a nature full of
simplicity, modesty, and benevolence. His industry
is, of itself, exhilarating to contemplate.

During the whole preceding year, I had heard
Mr. Livingston's name, almost daily, in connexion
with his extremely difficult negotiations between
the United States and France,—or rather between
President Jackson and Louis Philippe. I had read
his despatches, (some of which were made public
that were never designed to be so,) and had not

been quite satisfied as to their straightforwardness, but concluded, on the whole, that he had done as much as human wits could well do in so absurd, and perplexed, and dangerous a quarrel, where the minister had to manage the temper of his own potentate, as well as baffle the policy of the European monarch. A desire for peace and justice was evident through the whole of Mr. Livingston's correspondence; and under all, a strong wish to get home. Here he was,—now ploughing his way up his own beloved river, whose banks were studded with the country-seats of a host of his relations. He came to me on the upper deck, and sat looking very placid, with his staff between his knees, and his strong, observing countenance melting into an expression of pleasure when he described to me his enjoyment in burying himself among the mountains of Switzerland. He said he would not now hear of mountains anywhere else,—at least not in either his own country or mine. He gave me some opinions upon the government of the King of the French, which I little expected to hear from the minister of a democratic republic. We were deep in this subject, when a great hissing of the steam made us look up and see that we were at Hyde Park, and that Dr. Hosack and a party of ladies were waiting for me on the wharf.—I repeatedly met Mr. Livingston in society in New York, the next spring, when a deafness, which had been slight, was growing upon him, and impairing his enjoyment of conversation. The last time I saw him was at the christening of a grand-niece, when he looked well in health, but conversed little, and seemed rather out of spirits. Within a month of that evening, he was seized with pleurisy, which would in all probability have yielded to treatment; but he refused medicine, and was carried off, after a very short illness.—Dr. Hosack died some months before him. How little did I think, as I now went from the one to the other, that both these vigorous old men would be laid in their graves, even before my return home should call upon me to bid them farewell!

The aspect of Hyde Park from the river had disappointed me, after all I had heard of it. It looks little more than a white house upon a ridge. I was therefore doubly delighted when I found what this ridge really was. It is a natural terrace, over-hanging one of the sweetest reaches of the river; and, though broad and straight at the top, not square and formal, like an artificial embankment, but undulating, sloping, and sweeping, between the ridge and the river, and dropped with trees; the whole carpeted with turf, tempting grown people, who happen to have the spirits of children, to run up and down the slopes, and play hide-and-seek in the hollows. Whatever we might be talking of as we paced the terrace, I felt a perpetual inclination to start off for play. Yet, when the ladies and ourselves actually did something like it, threading the little thickets, and rounding every promontory, even to the farthest, (which they call Cape Horn,) I felt that the possession of such a place ought to make a man devout, if any of the gifts of Providence can do so. To hold in one's hand that which melts all strangers' hearts is to be a steward in a very serious sense of the term. Most liberally did Dr. Hosack dispense the means of enjoyment he possessed. Hospitality is inseparably connected with his name in the minds of all who ever heard it: and it was hospitality of the heartiest and most gladsome kind.

Dr. Hosack had a good library,—I believe, one of the best private libraries in the country; some good pictures, and botanical and mineralogical cabinets of value. Among the ornaments of his house, I observed some biscuits and vases once belonging to Louis XVI., purchased by Dr. Hosack from a gentleman who had them committed to his keeping during the troubles of the first French Revolution.

In the afternoon, Dr. Hosack drove me in his gig round his estate, which lies on both sides of the high road; the farm on one side, and the pleasure grounds on the other. The conservatory is remarkable for America; and the flower-garden all that it can be made under present circumstances, but the neigh-

bouring country people have no idea of a gentleman's
pleasure in his garden, and of respecting it.   On
occasions of weddings and other festivities, the vil-
lagers come up into the Hyde Park grounds to enjoy
themselves; and persons, who would not dream of
any other mode of theft, pull up rare plants, as they
would wild flowers in the woods, and carry them
away.   Dr. Hosack would frequently see some
flower that he had brought with much pains from
Europe flourishing in some garden of the village
below.   As soon as he explained the nature of
the case, the plant would be restored with all zeal
and care: but the losses were so frequent and
provoking as greatly to moderate his horticultural
enthusiasm.   We passed through the poultry-yard,
where the congregation of fowls exceeded in number
and bustle any that I had ever seen.   We drove
round his kitchen-garden too, where he had taken
pains to grow every kind of vegetable which will
flourish in that climate.   Then crossing the road,
after paying our respects to his dairy of fine cows,
we drove through the orchard, and round Cape
Horn, and refreshed ourselves with the sweet river
views on our way home.   There we sat in the pa-
vilion, and he told me much of De Witt Clinton,
and showed me his own Life of Clinton, a copy of
which he said should await me on my return to New
York.   When that time came, he was no more; but

his promise was kindly borne in mind by his lady, from whose hands I received the valued legacy.

We saw some pleasant society at Hyde Park: among the rest, some members of the wide-spreading Livingston family, and the Rev. Charles Stewart, who lived for some years as missionary in the South Sea Islands, and afterwards published a very interesting account of his residence there. His manners, which are particularly gentlemanly and modest, show no traces of a residence among savages, or of the shifts and disorder of a missionary life; nor of any bad effects from the sudden fame which awaited him on his return into civilized life. I remember with great pleasure a conversation we had by the river-side, which proved to me that he understands the philosophy of fame, knowing how to appropriate the good and reject the evil that it brings, and which deepened the respect I had entertained for him from the beginning of our acquaintance.

The Livingston family, one of the oldest, most numerous, and opulent in the States, has been faithful in the days of its greatness to its democratic principles. In Boston it seems a matter of course that the " first people" should be federalists; that those who may be aristocratic in station should become aristocratic in principle. The Livingstons are an evidence that this need not be. Amidst their splendid entertainments in New York, and in their luxu-

rious retirements on the Hudson, they may be heard
going further than most in defence of President
Jackson's idiosyncracy. Their zeal in favour of Mr.
Van Buren was accounted for by many from the
natural bias of the first family in the State of New
York in favour of the first President furnished by
that State: but there is no reason to find any such
cause. The Livingstons have consistently advocated
the most liberal principles, through all changes;
and that they retain their democratic opinions in the
midst of their opulence and family influence is not
the less honourable to them for their party having
now the ascendancy.

Dr. Hosack and his family accompanied us down
to the wharf, to see Mr. Stewart off by one boat,
and our party by another, when, on the third day of
our visit, we were obliged to depart. Our hearts
would have been more sorrowful than they were, if
we had foreseen that we should not enjoy our promised meeting with this accomplished and amiable
family at New York.

Dr. Hosack was a native American, but his father
was Scotch. After obtaining the best medical education he could in America, he studied in Edinburgh
and London: and hence his affectionate relations
with Great Britain, and the warmth with which he
welcomed English travellers. He practised medicine in New York for upwards of forty years, and

filled the Professorship of Botany and Materia Medica in Columbia College for some time. He distinguished himself by his successful attention to the causes and treatment of yellow fever. But his services out of his profession were as eminent as any for which his fellow-citizens are indebted to him. He rendered liberal aid to various literary, scientific and benevolent institutions, and was always willing and indefatigable in exertion for public objects. One of the most painful scenes of his life was the duel in which Hamilton perished. Dr. Hosack was Hamilton's second, and probably as well aware as his principal and others that the encounter could hardly end otherwise than as it did. Dr. Hosack was in New York with his family, the winter after my visit to Hyde Park. He was one day in medical conversation with Dr. McVickar of that city, and observed that it would not do for either of them to have an attack of apoplexy, as there would be small chance of their surviving it. Within two weeks both were dead of apoplexy. Dr. Hosack lost property in the great fire at New York; he over-exerted himself on the night of the fire; and the fatigue and anxiety brought on an attack of the disease he dreaded; under which he presently sank from amidst the well-earned enjoyments of a vigorous and prosperous old age. He was in his 67th year, and showed, to the eye of a stranger, no symptom of decline. His eye was bright, his spirits as buoyant, and his life as full of activity as those of most men of half his years.   I always heard the death of this enterprising and useful citizen mentioned as heading the list of the calamities of the Great Fire.

PINE ORCHARD HOUSE.

" But the new glory mixes with the heaven
  And earth. Man, once descried, imprints for ever
  His presence on all lifeless things—the winds
  Are henceforth voices, wailing or a shout,
  A querulous mutter or a quick gay laugh—
  Never a senseless gust now Man is born.
  The herded pines commune, and have deep thoughts,
  A secret they assemble to discuss,
  When the sun drops behind their trunks which glare
  Like grates of hell: the peerless cup afloat
  Of the lake-lily is an urn some nymph
  Swims bearing high above her head.
         *   *   *   *   *   *   *
  The morn has enterprise ;—deep quiet droops
  With evening ;—triumph when the sun takes rest ;—
  Voluptuous transport when the corn-fields ripen
  Beneath a warm moon, like a happy face :
  And this to fill us with regard for Man,
  Deep apprehension of his passing worth."
                                Paracelsus, part v.

HOWEVER widely European travellers have differed
about other things in America, all seem to agree in
their love of the Hudson. The pens of all tourists
dwell on its scenery, and their affections linger about
it, like the magical lights which seem to have this
river in their peculiar charge. Yet very few travellers have seen its noblest wonder. I may be singular ; but I own that I was more moved by what I

saw from the Mountain House than by Niagara itself.

What is this Mountain House,—this Pine Orchard House? many will ask; for its name is not to be found in most books of American travels. "What is that white speck?" I myself asked, when staying at Tivoli, on the east bank of the Hudson, opposite to the Catskills, whose shadowy surface was perpetually tempting the eye. That white speck, visible to most eyes only when bright sunshine was upon it, was the Mountain House,—a hotel built for the accommodation of hardy travellers who may desire to obtain that complete view of the valley of the Hudson which can be had nowhere else. I made up my mind to go; and the next year I went, on leaving Dr. Hosack's. I think I had rather have missed the Hawk's Nest, the Prairies, the Mississippi, and even Niagara, than this.

The steam-boat in which we left Hyde Park landed us at Catskill (31 miles) at a little after three in the afternoon. Stages were waiting to convey passengers to the Mountain House; and we were off in a few minutes, expecting to perform the ascending journey of twelve miles in a little more than four hours. We had the same horses all the way, and therefore set off at a moderate pace, though the road was for some time level, intersecting rich bottoms, and passing flourishing farm-houses, where the men were milking, and the women looked up from their work in the piazzas as we passed. Haymaking was going on in fields which appeared to hang above us at first, but on which we afterwards looked down from such a height that the haycocks were scarcely distinguishable. It was the 25th of July, and a very hot day for the season. The roads were parched up, and every exposed thing that one handled on board the steam-boat, or in the stage, made one flinch from the burning sensation. The panting horses, one of them bleeding at the mouth, stopped to drink at a house at the foot of the ascent; and we wondered how, exhausted as they seemed, they would drag us up the mountain. We did not calculate on the change of temperature which we were soon to experience.

The mountain laurel conveyed by association the first impression of coolness. Sheep were browsing among the shrubs, apparently enjoying the shelter of the covert. We scrambled through deep shade for three or four miles, heavy showers passing over us, and gusts of wind bowing the tree tops, and sending a shiver through us, partly from the sudden chillness, and partly from expectation, and awe of the breezy solitude. On turning a sharp angle of the steep road, at a great elevation, we stopped in a damp green nook, where there was an arrangement of hollow trees to serve for water-troughs. While the horses were drinking, the gusts parted the trees, to the left, and disclosed to me a vast extent of country lying below, chequered with light and shadow. This was the moment in which a lady in the stage said with a yawn, " I hope we shall find something at the top to pay us for all this." Truly the philosophy of recompense seems to be little understood. In moral affairs, people seem to expect recompense for privileges; as when children, grown and ungrown, are told that they will be rewarded for doing their duty: and here was a lady hoping for recompense for being carried up a glorious mountain side, in ease, coolness, leisure, and society, all at once. If it was recompense for the evil of inborn *ennui* that she wanted, she was not likely to find it where she was going to look for it.

After another level reach of road, and another scrambling ascent, I saw something on the rocky platform above our heads, like (to compare great things with small) an illumined fairy palace perched among clouds in opera scenery;—a large building, whose numerous window-lights marked out its figure from amidst the thunder-clouds and black twilight which overshadowed it. It was now half-past eight o'clock, and a stormy evening. Everything was chill, and we were glad of lights and tea in the first place.

After tea, I went out upon the platform in front

of the house, having been warned not to go too near the edge, so as to fall an unmeasured depth into the forest below. I sat upon the edge, as a security against stepping over unawares. The stars were bright overhead, and had conquered half the sky, giving promise of what we ardently desired, a fine morrow. Over the other half, the mass of thunder-clouds was, I supposed, heaped together, for I could at first discern nothing of the champaign which I knew must be stretched below. Suddenly, and from that moment incessantly, gushes of red lightning poured out from the cloudy canopy, revealing, not merely the horizon, but the course of the river, in all its windings through the valley. This thread of river, thus illuminated, looked like a flash of light-ning, caught by some strong hand, and laid along in the valley. All the principal features of the landscape might, no doubt, have been discerned by this sulphurous light; but my whole attention was absorbed by the river, which seemed to come out of the darkness, like an apparition, at the summons of my impatient will. It could be borne only for a short time,—this dazzling, bewildering alternation of glare and blackness, of vast reality and nothingness. I was soon glad to draw back from the precipice, and seek the candle-light within.

The next day was Sunday. I shall never forget, if I live to a hundred, how the world lay at my feet

one Sunday morning. I rose very early, and looked
abroad from my window,—two stories above the
platform. A dense fog, exactly level with my eyes,
as it appeared, roofed in the whole plain of the
earth; a dusky firmament in which the stars had
hidden themselves for the day. Such is the account
which an antediluvian spectator would probably
have given of it. This solid firmament had spaces
in it, however, through which gushes of sunlight
were poured, lighting up the spires of white churches,
and clusters of farm buildings too small to be otherwise distinguished; and especially the river, with its
sloops, floating like motes in the sunbeam. The
firmament rose and melted; or parted off into the
likeness of snowy sky-mountains, and left the cool
Sabbath to brood brightly over the land. What
human interest sanctifies a bird's eye view! I
suppose this is its peculiar charm; for its charm is
found to deepen in proportion to the growth of
mind. To an infant, a champaign of a hundred
miles is not so much as a yard square of gay carpet.
To the rustic, it is less bewitching than a paddock
with two cows. To the philosopher, what is it not?
As he casts his eye over its glittering towns, its
scattered hamlets, its secluded homes, its mountain
ranges, church spires, and untrodden forests, it is a
picture of life; an epitome of the human universe;
the complete volume of moral philosophy for which

he has sought in vain in all libraries. On the left horizon are the green mountains of Vermont; and at the right extremity sparkles the Atlantic. Beneath lies the forest where the deer are hiding, and the birds rejoicing in song. Beyond the river, he sees spread the rich plains of Connecticut: there, where a blue expanse lies beyond the triple range of hills, are the churches of religious Massachusetts sending up their Sabbath psalms,—praise which he is too high to hear, while God is not. The fields and waters seem to him to-day no more truly property than the skies which shine down upon them; and to think how some below are busying their thoughts this Sabbath-day about how they shall hedge in another field, or multiply their flocks on yonder meadows, gives him a taste of the same pity which Jesus felt in his solitude when his followers were contending about which should be greatest. It seems strange to him now that man should call anything *his* but the power which is in him, and which can create somewhat more vast and beautiful than all that this horizon encloses. Here he gains the conviction, to be never again shaken, that all that is real is ideal; that the joys and sorrows of men do not spring up out of the ground, or fly abroad on the wings of the wind, or come showered down from the sky; that good cannot be hedged in, nor evil barred out; even that light does not reach

the spirit through the eye alone, nor wisdom through
the medium of sound or silence only.   He becomes
of one mind with the spiritual Berkeley, that the
face of nature itself, the very picture of woods and
streams and meadows, is a hieroglyphic writing in
the spirit itself, of which the retina is no interpreter.
The proof is just below him, (at least it came under
my eye,) in the lady (not American) who, after
glancing over the landscape, brings her chair into
the piazza, and turning her back to the champaign,
and her face to the wooden walls of the hotel,
begins the study, this Sunday morning, of her lap-
full of newspapers.   What a sermon is thus preached
to him at this moment, from a very hackneyed text!
To him that hath much,—that hath the eye and ear
and wealth of the spirit, shall more be given,—even
a replenishing of this spiritual life from that which
to others is formless and dumb: while from him
that hath little, who trusts in that which lies about
him rather than in that which lives within him, shall
be taken away, by natural decline, the power of
perceiving and enjoying what is within his own
domain.   To him who is already enriched with
large divine and human revelations, this scene is,
for all its stillness, musical with divine and human
speech: while one who has been deafened by the
din of worldly affairs can hear nothing in this
mountain solitude.

The march of the day over the valley was glorious, and I was grieved to have to leave my window for an expedition to the Falls, a few miles off. The Falls are really very fine,—or rather their environment; but I could see plenty of waterfalls elsewhere; but nowhere else such a mountain platform. However, the expedition was a good preparation for the return to my window. The little nooks of the road, crowded with bilberries, cherries, and alpine plants, and the quiet tarn, studded with golden water-lilies, were a wholesome contrast to the grandeur of what we had left behind us.

On returning, we found dinner awaiting us, and also a party of friends out of Massachusetts, with whom we passed the afternoon, climbing higher and higher, among the pines, ferns, and blue-berries of the mountain, to get wider and wider views. They told me that I saw Albany; but I was by no means sure of it. This large city lay in the landscape like an anthill in a meadow. Long before sunset, I was at my window again, watching the gradual lengthening of the shadows and purpling of the landscape. It was more beautiful than the sunrise of this morning, and less so than that of the morrow. Of this last, I shall give no description; for I would not weary others with what is most sacred to me. Suffice it that it gave me a vivid idea of the process of creation, from the moment when all was without form

and void to that when light was commanded, and
there was light. Here again I was humbled by
seeing what such things are to some who watch in
vain for what they are not made to see.—A gentleman and lady in the hotel intended to have left the
place on Sunday. Having overslept that morning's
sunrise, and arrived too late for that on Saturday,
they were persuaded to stay till Monday noon;
and I was pleased, on rising at four on Monday
morning, to see that they were in the piazza below,
with a telescope. We met at breakfast, all faint
with hunger, of course.

"Well, Miss M.," said the gentleman, discon-
tentedly, " I suppose you were disappointed in the
sunrise."

" No, I was not."

" Why, do you think the sun was any handsomer
here than at New York?"

I made no answer; for what could one say? But
he drove me by questions to tell what I expected to
see in the sun.

" I did not expect to see the sun green or blue."

" What did you expect then?"

I was obliged to explain that it was the effect of
the sun on the landscape that I had been looking for.

" Upon the landscape! O! but we saw that
yesterday."

The gentleman was perfectly serious, — quite

earnest in all this. When we were departing, a foreign tourist was heard to complain of the high charges! High charges! As if we were to be supplied for nothing on a perch where the wonder is if any but the young ravens get fed! When I considered what a drawback it is in visiting mountain-tops that one is driven down again almost immediately by one's bodily wants, I was ready to thank the people devoutly for harbouring us on any terms, so that we might think out our thoughts, and compose our emotions, and take our fill of that portion of our universal and eternal inheritance.

WEDDINGS.

"God, the best maker of all marriages,
Combine your hearts in one!"
Henry V.

I WAS present at four weddings in the United States, and at an offer of marriage.

The offer of marriage ought hardly to be so called, however. It was a petition from a slave to be allowed to wed (as slaves wed) the nursemaid of a lady in whose house I was staying. The young man could either write a little, or had employed some one who could, to prepare his epistle for him. It ran from corner to corner of the paper, which was daubed with diluted wafer, like certain love-letters nearer home than Georgia. Here are the contents :—

"Miss Cunningham it is My wishes to companion in your Present and I hope you will Be peeze at it and I hope that you will not think Hard of Me I have Ben to the Doctor and he was very well satafide with Me and I hope you is and Miss Mahuw all so

"thats all I has to say now wiheshen you will grant Me that honor I will Be very glad.

"S. B. SMITH."

The nursemaid was granted : and as it was a love-match, and as the girl's mistress is one of the tender —the sore-hearted about having slaves, I hope the poor creatures are as happy as love in debasement can make them.

The first wedding I saw in Boston was very like the common run of weddings in England. It happened to be convenient that the parties should be married in church; and in the Unitarian church in which they usually worshipped we accordingly awaited them. I had no acquaintance with the family, but went on the invitation of the pastor who married them. The family connexion was large, and the church therefore about half full. The form of celebration is at the pleasure of the pastor ; but by consent the administration by pastors of the same sect is very nearly alike. The promises of the married parties are made reciprocal, I observed. The service in this instance struck me as being very beautiful from its simplicity, tenderness, and brevity. There was one variation from the usual method, in the offering of one of the prayers by a second pastor, who, being the uncle of the bridegroom, was invited to take a share in the service.

The young people were to set out for Europe in the afternoon, the bride being out of health,—the dreary drawback upon almost every extensive plan of action and fair promise of happiness in America.

The lady has, I rejoice to hear, been quite restored by travel; but her sickness threw a gloom over the celebration, even in the minds of strangers. She and her husband walked up the middle aisle to the desk where the pastors sat. They were attended by only one bride's-maid and one groom's-man, and were all in plain travelling dresses. They said steadily and quietly what they had to say, and walked down the aisle again as they came. Nothing could be simpler and better ; for this was not a marriage where festivity could have place. If there is any natural scope for joy, let weddings, by all means, be joyous; but here there was sickness, with the prospect of a long family separation, and there was most truth in quietness.

The other wedding I saw in Boston was as gay an one as is often seen. The parties were opulent, and in the first rank of society. They were married in the drawing-room of the bride's house, at half-past eight in the evening, by Dr. Channing. The moment the ceremony was over, crowds of company began to arrive; and the bride, young and delicate, and her maidens, were niched in a corner of one of the drawing-rooms, to curtsey to all comers. They were so formally placed, so richly and (as it then seemed) formally dressed,—for the present revived antique style of dress was then quite new,— that, in the interval of their curtseys, they looked

like an old picture brought from Windsor Castle.
The bride's mother presided in the other drawing-
room, and the bridegroom flitted about, universally
attentive, and on the watch to introduce all visitors
to his lady. The transition from the solemnity
of Dr. Channing's service to the noisy gaieties
of a rout was not at all to my taste. I imagined
that it was not to Dr. Channing's either, for his talk
with me was on matters very little resembling anything that we had before our eyes: and he soon
went away. The noise became such as to silence
all who were not inured to the gabble of an American party,—the noisiest kind of assemblage, I
imagine, (not excepting a Jew's synagogue,) on the
face of the globe. I doubt whether any Pagans in
their worship can raise any hubbub to equal it. I
constantly found in a large party, after trying in vain
every kind of scream that I was capable of, that I
must give up, and satisfy myself with nodding and
shaking my head. If I was rightly understood, well
and good: if not, I must let it pass.—As the noise
thickened and the heat grew more oppressive, I
glanced towards the poor bride in her corner, still
standing, still curtseying; her pale face growing
paler; her nonchalant manner (perhaps the best
she could assume) more indifferent. I was afraid
that if all this went on much longer, she would faint
or die upon the spot. It did not last much longer.

By eleven, some of the company began to go away, and by a quarter before twelve all were gone but the comparatively small party (including ourselves) who were invited to stay to supper.

The chandelier and mantelpieces, I then saw, were dressed with flowers. There was a splendid supper; and before we departed, we were carried up to a large well-lighted apartment, where bride cake and the wedding presents were set out in bright array.

Five days afterwards we went, in common with all her acquaintance, to pay our respects to the bride. The court-yard of her mother's house was thronged with carriages, though no one seemed to stay five minutes. The bridegroom received us at the head of the stairs, and led us to his lady, who curtseyed as before. Cake, wine, and liqueurs were handed round, the visitors all standing. A few words on common subjects were exchanged, and we were gone, to make way for others.

A Quaker marriage which I witnessed at Philadelphia was scarcely less showy in its way. It took place at the Cherry Street church, belonging to the Hicksites. The reformed Quaker Church, consisting of the followers of Elias Hicks, bears about the same relation to the old Quakerism as the Church of England to that of Rome; and, it seems to me, the mutual dislike is as intense. I question whether religious enmity ever attained a greater extreme than among the orthodox Friends of Philadelphia. The Hicksites are more moderate, but are sometimes naturally worried out of their patience, by the meddling, the denunciations, and the calumnies of the old Quaker societies. The new church is thinking of reforming and relaxing a good deal further; and in the celebration of marriage among other things. It is under consideration, (or was when I was there) whether the process of betrothment should not be simplified, and marriage in the father's house permitted to such as prefer it to the church. The wedding at which I was present was, however, performed with all the formalities.

A Quaker friend of mine, a frequent preacher, suggested, a few days previously, that a seat had better be reserved for me near the speakers, that I might have a chance of hearing, "in case there should be communications." I had hopes from this that my friend would speak; and my wishes were not disappointed.

The spacious church was crowded; and for three or four hours the poor bride had to sit facing the assemblage,—aware, doubtless, that during the time of silence, the occupation of the strangers present, if not of the friends themselves, would be watching her and her party. She was pretty, and most beautifully dressed. I have seldom pitied anybody more than I did her, while she sat palpitating for three hours under the gaze of some hundreds of people: but, towards the end of the time of silence, my compassion was transferred to the bridegroom. For want of something to do, after suppressing many yawns, he looked up to the ceiling; and in the midst of an empty stare, I imagine he caught the eye of an acquaintance in the back seats, for he was instantly troubled with a most irrepressible and unseasonable inclination to laugh. He struggled manfully with his difficulty; but the smiles would come, broader and broader. If, by dint of looking steadfastly into his hat for a few minutes, he attained a becoming gravity, it was gone the moment he raised his head. I was in a panic lest we should have a scandalous peal of merriment, if something was not given him to do, or listen to. Happily " there were communications," and the course of his ideas was changed.

Of the five speakers, one was an old gentleman whose discourse was an entire perplexity to me. For nearly an hour, he discoursed on Jacob's ladder; but in a style so rambling, and in a chant so singularly unmusical as to set attention and remembrance at defiance. Some parenthetical observations alone stood a chance of being retained, from their singularity;—one, for instance, which he introduced in the course of his narrative about Jacob setting a

stone for a pillow;—" a very different," cried the
preacher, raising his chant to the highest pitch,—
" a very different pillow, by the way, from any that
we—are—accommodated—with."—What a contrast
was the brief discourse of my Quaker friend which
followed! Her noble countenance was radiant as
the morning, her soft voice, though low, so firm that
she was heard to the furthest corner, and her little
sermon as philosophical as it was devout. " Send
forth thy light and thy truth," was her text. She
spoke gratefully of intellectual light as a guide to
spiritual truth, and anticipated and prayed for an
ultimate universal diffusion of both.—The certificate
of the marriage was read by Dr. Parrish, an elderly
physician of Philadelphia, the very realization of all
my imaginings of the personal appearance of Wil-
liam Penn; with all the dignity and bonhommie
that one fancies Penn invested with in his dealings
with the Indians. Dr. Parrish speaks with affection
of the Indians, from the experience some ancestors
of his had of the hospitality of these poor people,
when they were in a condition to show hospitality.
His grandfather's family were shipwrecked; and
the Indians took the poor lady and her children
home to an inhabited cave, and fed them for many
weeks or months. The tree stump round which
they used to sit at meals is still standing; and Dr.
Parrish says that, let it stand as long as it will, the
love of his family to the Indians shall outlast it.

The matrimonial promise was distinctly and well spoken by both the parties. At the request of the bride and bridegroom, Dr. Parrish asked me to put the first signature, after their own, to the certificate of the marriage; and we adjourned for the purpose to an apartment connected with the church. Most ample sheets of parchment were provided for the signatures, and there was a prodigious array of names before we left, when a crowd was still waiting to testify. This multitudinous witnessing is the pleasantest part of being married by acclamation. If weddings are not to be private, there seems no question of the superiority of this Quaker method to that of the Boston marriage I witnessed, where there was all the publicity, without the co-operation and sanction.

The last wedding which I have to give an account of is full of a melancholy interest to me now. All was so joyous, so simple, so right, that there seemed no suggestion to evil-boding, no excuse for anticipating such woe as has followed.— On one of the latter days of July, 1835, I reached the village of Stockbridge,—the Sedgwicks' village,—for the second time, intending to stay four or five days with my friends there. I had heard of an approaching wedding in the family connexion, and was glad that I had planned to leave, so as to be out of the way at a time when I supposed the presence of foreigners, though friends, might be easily dispensed with.

But when Miss Sedgwick and I were sitting in her room, one bright morning, there was a tap at the door. It was the pretty black-eyed girl who was to be married the next week. She stood only a minute on the threshold to say, with grave simplicity, " I am come to ask you to join our friends at my father's house, next Tuesday evening." Being thus invited, I joyfully assented, and put off my journey.

The numerous children of the family connexion were in wild spirits all that Tuesday. In the morning, we went a strong party to the Ice Hole,—a defile between two hills, so perplexed and encumbered with rocks that none but practised climbers need attempt the passage. It was a good way for the young people to work off their exuberant spirits. Their laughter was heard from amidst the nooks and hiding-places of the labyrinth, and smiling faces might be seen behind every shrubby screen which sprang up from the crevices. How we tried to surpass each other in the ferns and mosses we gathered, rich in size and variety! What skipping and scrambling there was ; what trunk bridges, and ladders of roots ! How valiant the ladies looked with their stout sticks ! How glad every one was to feast upon the wild raspberries when we struggled through the close defile into the cool, green, breezy meadow on the banks of the Housatonic !—During the afternoon, we were very quiet, reading one of

Carlyle's reviews aloud (for the wentieth time, I
believe, to some of the party), and discussing it and
other things.   By eight o'clock, we were all dressed
for the wedding, and some of the children ran over
the green before us, but came back, saying that all
was not quite ready : so we got one of the girls to
sing to us for another half hour.

The house of the bride's father was well lighted,
and dressed with flowers.   She had no mother ; but
her elder sisters aided their father in bidding us welcome.   The drawing-room was quite full ; and
while the grown-up friends found it difficult to talk,
and to repress the indefinable anxiety and agitation
which always attend a wedding, the younger members of the party were amusing themselves with
whispered mirth.   The domestics looked as if the
most joyous event of their lives were taking place,
and the old father seemed placid and satisfied.

In a few minutes, we were summoned to another
room, at the top of which stood the tall bridegroom,
with his pretty little lady on his arm ; on either side,
the three gentlemen and three ladies who attended
them ; and in front the episcopalian minister who
was to marry them, and who has since been united
to one of the sisters.   It was the first time of his per-
forming the ceremony ; and his manner was solemn
and somewhat anxious, as might be expected.

The bridegroom was a professor in a college in

the neighbouring State of New York; a young man of high acquirements and character, to whom the old father might well be proud to give his daughter. His manners were remarkably pleasing, and there was a joyous, dignified serenity visible in them this evening which at once favourably prepossessed us, who did not previously know him. He was attended by a brother professor from the same college.—When the service was over, we all kissed the grave and quiet bride. I trust that no bodings of the woes which awaited her cast a shadow over her spirits then. I think, though grave, she was not sad. She spoke with all her father's guests in the course of the evening, as did her husband. How often have I of late tried to recal precisely what they said to me, and every look with which they said it!

We went back to the drawing room for cake and wine: and then ensued the search for the ring in the great wedding cake, with much merriment among those who were alive to all the fun of a festivity like this, and to none of the care. There was much moving about between the rooms, and dressing with flowers in the hall; and lively conversation,—as it must needs be where there are Sedgwicks. Then champagne and drinking of healths went round, the guests poured out upon the green, all the ladies with handkerchiefs tied

over their heads.   There we bade good night, and
parted off to our several homes.

When I left the village, the next morning, two
or three carriages full of young people were setting
off, as attendants upon the bride and bridegroom,
to Lebanon.   After a few such short excursions in
the neighbourhood, the young couple went home
to begin their quiet college and domestic life.

Before a year had elapsed,—a year which to me
seemed gone like a month,—I was at Stockbridge
again, and found the young wife's family in great
trouble.   She was in a raging fever, consequent on
her confinement, and great fears were entertained
for her life.   Her infant seemed to have but a
small chance, under the circumstances; and there
was a passing mention of her husband being ill.
Every one spoke of him with a respect and affection
which showed how worthy he was of this young
creature's love ; and it was our feeling for him
which made our prayers for her restoration so
earnest as they were.   The last I heard of her
before I left the country was that she was slowly
and doubtfully recovering, but had not yet been
removed from her father's house.—The next intelligence that I received, after my return to England,
was of her husband's death :—that he had died in a
calm and satisfied state of mind; satisfied that if
their reasonable hopes of domestic joy and useful-

ness had not been fulfilled, it was for wise and kind reasons; and that the strong hand which thus early divided them would uphold the gentle survivor. No one who witnessed and blessed their union can help beseeching and trusting, since all other hope is over, that it may be even thus.

HIGH ROAD TRAVELLING.

" How far my pen has been fatigued like those of other travellers, in this journey of it—the world must judge—but the traces of it, which are now all set o'vibrating together this moment, tell me it is the most fruitful and busy period of my life; for, as I had made no convention with my man with the gun as to time—by seizing every handle, of what size or shape soever which chance held out to me in this journey—I was always in company, and with great variety too."—*Sterne.*

OUR first land travelling, in which we had to take our chance with the world in general, was across the State of New York. My account of what we saw may seem excessively minute in some of its details; but this style of particularity is not adopted without reasons. While writing my journal, I always endeavoured to bear in mind the rapidity with which civilization advances in America, and the desirableness of recording things precisely in their present state, in order to have materials for comparison some few years hence, when travelling may probably be as unlike what it is now, as a journey from London to Liverpool by the new railroad differs from the same enterprise as undertaken a century and a half ago.

To avoid some of the fatigues and liabilities of

common travelling, certain of our shipmates and their friends, and ourselves had made up a party to traverse the State of New York in an "exclusive extra;" a stage hired, with the driver, for our own use, to proceed at our own time. Our fellow-travellers were a German and a Dutch gentleman, and the Prussian physician and young South Carolinian whom I have mentioned in the list of our shipmates. We were to meet at the Congress Hall hotel in Albany, on the 6th of October.

On our way from Stockbridge to Albany, we saw a few objects characteristic of the country. While the horses were baiting, we wandered into a graveyard, where the names on the tombstones were enough to inform any observer what country of the world he was in. One inscription was laudatory of Nelson and Nabby Bullis : another of Amasa and Polly Fielding. Hiram and Keziah were there too. The signs in the American streets are as ludicrous for their confusion of Greek, Roman and Hebrew names as those of Irish towns are for the arbitrary divisions of words. One sees Rudolphus figuring beside Eliakim, and Aristides beside Zerug. I pitied an acquaintance of mine for being named Peleg, till I found he had baptized his two boys Peleg and Seth.—On a table in a little wayside inn, I found Fox's Martyrs; and against the wall hung a framed sampler, with the following lines worked upon it.

"Jesus, permit thine awful name to stand
As the first offering of an infant's hand:
And as her fingers o'er the canvass move,
O fill her thoughtful bosom with thy love.
With thy dear children let her bear a part,
And write thy name thyself upon her heart."

In these small inns the disagreeable practice of rocking in the chair is seen in its excess. In the inn parlour are three or four rocking chairs, in which sit ladies who are vibrating in different directions, and at various velocities, so as to try the head of a stranger almost as severely as the tobacco chewer his stomach. How this lazy and ungraceful indulgence ever became general, I cannot imagine; but the nation seems so wedded to it, that I see little chance of its being forsaken. When American ladies come to live in Europe, they sometimes send home for a rocking-chair. A common wedding present is a rocking-chair. A beloved pastor has every room in his house furnished with a rocking-chair by his grateful and devoted people. It is well that the gentlemen can be satisfied to sit still, or the world might be treated with the spectacle of the sublime American Senate in a new position; its fifty-two senators see-sawing in full deliberation, like the wise birds of a rookery in a breeze. If such

a thing should ever happen, it will be time for them
to leave off laughing at the Shaker worship.

As we approached Greenbush, which lies opposite to Albany, on the east bank of the Hudson, we
met riding-horses, exercised by grooms, and more
than one handsome carriage,—tokens that we were
approaching some centre of luxury. The view of
Albany rising from the river side, with its brown-
stone court-house and white marble capitol, is fine;
but it wants the relief of more trees within itself, or
of a rural back-ground. How changed is this bust-
ling city, thronged with costly buildings, from the
Albany of the early days of Mrs. Grant of Laggan,
when the children used to run up and down the
green slope which is now State Street,—imposing
from its width, and the massiveness of the houses
seen behind its rows of trees! A tunnel is about
to be made under the Hudson at Albany; meantime we crossed, as every body does, by a horse-
ferry boat; a device so cruel, as well as clumsy,
that the sooner it is superseded the better. I was
told that the strongest horses, however kept up with
corn, rarely survive a year of this work.

We observed that, even in this city, the physicians
have not always their names engraved on brass
door-plates. On the most conspicuous part of
their houses,—perhaps on the angle of a corner
house,—is nailed some glazed substance like floor-

cloth, with " Dr. Such-an-one " painted upon it.
At Washington I remember seeing " MAGISTRATE "
thus affixed to a mere shed.

As we surmounted the hill leading to our hotel,
we saw our two shipmates dancing down the steps
to welcome us.   There certainly is a feeling among
shipmates which does not grow out of any other
relation.   They are thrown first into such absolute
dependence on one another, for better for worse, and
are afterwards so suddenly and widely separated,
that if they do chance to meet again, they renew
their intimacy with a fervour which does not belong
to a friendship otherwise originated.   The glee of
our whole party this evening is almost ridiculous to
look back upon.   Everything served to make a
laugh, and we were almost intoxicated with the
prospect of what we were going to see and do together.   We had separated only a fortnight ago; but
we had as much to talk over as if we had been
travelling apart for six months.   The Prussian had
to tell his adventures; we our impressions; and the
Southerner his comparisons of his own country with
Europe.   Then we had to arrange the division
of labour by which the gentlemen were to lighten
the cares of travelling.   Dr. J., the Prussian, was
on all occasions to select apartments for us; Mr.
S., the Dutchman, to undertake the eating department; Mr. H., the American, was paymaster, and

Mr. O., the German, took charge of the luggage. It was proposed that badges should be worn to designate their offices. Mr. S. was to be adorned with a corn cob. Mr. H. stuck a bank bill in front of his hat; and, next morning, when Mr. O. was looking another way, the young men locked a small padlock upon his button-hole, which he was compelled to carry there for a day or two till his comrades vouchsafed to release him from his badge.

The hotel was well furnished and conducted. I pointed out, with some complacency, what a handsome piano we had in our drawing-room ; but when, in the dark hour, I opened it in order to play, I found it empty of keys !—a disappointment, however, which I have met with in England.

Mr. Van Buren and his son happened to be in Albany, and called on me this afternoon. There is nothing remarkable in the appearance of this gentleman, whom I afterwards saw frequently at Washington. He is small in person, with light hair, and blue eyes. I was often asked whether I did not think his manners gentlemanly. There is much friendliness in his manners, for he is a kind-hearted man : he is also rich in information, and lets it come out on subjects in which he cannot contrive to see any danger in speaking. But his manners want the frankness and confidence which are essential to good breeding. He questions closely without giving anything in return. Moreover, he flatters to a degree which so cautious a man should long ago have found out to be disagreeable: and his flattery is not merely praise of the person he is speaking to, but a worse kind still,—a scepticism and ridicule of objects and persons supposed to be distasteful to the one he is conversing with. I fully believe that he is an amiable and indulgent domestic man, and a reasonable political master, a good scholar, and a shrewd man of business: but he has the scepticism which marks the lower orders of politicians. His public career exhibits no one exercise of that faith in men, and preference of principle to petty expediency by which a statesman shows himself to be great.

The consequence is that, with all his opportunities, no great deed has ever been put to his account, and his shrewdness has been at fault in some of the most trying crises of his career. The man who so little trusts others, and so intensely regards self as to make it the study of his life not to commit himself, is liable to a more than ordinary danger of judging wrong when compelled, by the pressure of circumstances, to act a decided part. It has already been so with Mr. Van Buren, more than once; and now that he is placed in a position where he must sometimes visibly lead, and cannot always appear to follow, it will be seen whether a due reverence of men and a forgetfulness of self would not have furnished him with more practical wisdom than all his " sounding on his dim and perilous way." Mr. Calhoun is, I believe, Mr. Van Buren's evil genius. Mr. Calhoun was understood to be in expectation of succeeding to the presidential chair when Mr. Van Buren was appointed Minister to Great Britain. This appointment of President Jackson's did not receive the necessary sanction from the Senate; and the new minister was recalled on the first possible day, Mr. Calhoun being very active in bringing him back. Mr. Calhoun was not aware that he was recalling one who was to prove a successful rival. Mr. Calhoun has not been President; Mr. Van Buren is so: but the successful rival has a mortal dread of the great Nullifier—a dread so obvious, and causing such a prostration of all principle and all dignity, as to oblige observers to conclude that there is more in the matter than they see; that it will come out some day why the disappointed aspirant is still to be propitiated, when he seems to be deprived of power to do mischief. In " Society in America " I have given an account of the Nullification struggle, and of the irritation, the mysterious discontent, which it has left behind *."

Perhaps Mr. Van Buren may entertain the opinion

* Society in America, vol. i., p. 91.

which many hold, that that business is not over yet,
and that the slavery question is made a pretext by
the Nullifiers of the South, for a line of action to
which they are impelled by the disappointed personal
ambition of one or two, and the wounded pride of
the many who cannot endure the contrast between
the increase of the Free States of the North and the
deterioration of the Slave States of the South. However this may be, to propitiate Mr. Calhoun seems
to have been Mr. Van Buren's great object for a
long time past : an object probably hopeless in itself,
and in the pursuit of which he is likely to lose the
confidence of the North far faster than he could, at
best, disarm the enmity of the South.

In the spring of 1836, when Mr. Van Buren
was still Vice-President, and the Presidential election was drawing near, Mr. Calhoun brought forward in the Senate his Bill, (commonly called the
Gag Bill,) to violate the post-office function, by au-
thorizing postmasters to investigate the contents of
the mails, and to keep back all papers whatsoever
relating to the subject of slavery. The Bill was,
by consent, read the first and second times without
debate ; and the Senate was to be divided on the
question whether it should go to a third reading.
The votes were equal,—18 to 18. " Where's the
Vice-President?" shouted Mr. Calhoun's mighty
voice. The Vice-President was behind a pillar,

talking. He was compelled to give the casting-vote,—to commit himself for once; a cruel necessity to a man of his caution. He voted for the third reading, and there was a bitter cry on the instant,—" The Northern States are sold." The Bill was thrown out on the division on the third reading, and the Vice-President lost by his vote the good-will of the whole body of abolitionists, who had till then supported him as the democratic and supposed anti-slavery candidate. As it was, most of the abolitionists did not vote at all, for want of a good candidate, and Mr. Van Buren's majority was so reduced as to justify a belief that if the people had had another year to consider his conduct in, or if another democratic candidate could have been put forward, he would have been emphatically rejected. Having once committed himself, he has gone further still, in propitiation of Mr. Calhoun. On the day of his presidential installation, he declared that under no circumstances would he give his assent to any bill for the abolition of slavery in the District of Columbia. This declaration does not arise out of a belief that Congress has not power to abolish slavery in the District; for he did, not long before, when hard pressed, declare that he believed Congress to possess that power. He has therefore hazarded the extraordinary declaration that he will not, under any circumstances, assent to what may become the will

of the people, constitutionally embodied.   This is a
bold intimation for a "non-committal man" to make.
It remains to be seen whether Mr. Calhoun, if really
dangerous, can be kept quiet by such fawning as
this; and whether the will of the people may not
be rather stimulated than restrained by this sacrifice
of them to the South, so as either to compel the
President to retract his declaration before his four
years are out, or to prevent his re-election.

How strange it is to recal one's first impressions
of public men in the midst of one's matured opinions
of them!   How freshly I remember the chat about
West Point and Stockbridge acquaintances that I
had that afternoon at Albany, with the conspicuous
man about whom I was then ignorant and indifferent,
and whom I have since seen committed to the lowest
political principles and practices, while elected as
professing some of the highest!   It only remains to
be said that if Mr. Van Buren feels himself aggrieved
by the interpretation which is commonly put upon
the facts of his political life, he has no one to blame
but himself; for such misinterpretation (if it exist)
is owing to his singular reserve; a reserve which all
men agree in considering incompatible with the
simple honesty, and cheerful admission of responsibility which democratic republicans have a right to
require of their rulers.

Before breakfast, the next morning, we walked

down to the Padroon's house,—known by reputation, with the history of the estate, to every body. We just caught a sight of the shrubbery, and took leave to pass through the court-yard, and hastened back to breakfast, immediately after which we proceeded by railroad to Schenectady. There we at once stepped into a canal-boat for Utica. I would never advise ladies to travel by canal, unless the boats are quite new and clean; or at least far better kept than any that I saw or heard of on this canal. On fine days it is pleasant enough sitting outside, (except for having to duck under the bridges, every quarter of an hour, under penalty of having one's head crushed to atoms,) and in dark evenings the approach of the boat-lights on the water is a pretty sight: but the horrors of night and of wet days more than compensate for all the advantages these vehicles can boast. The heat and noise, the known vicinity of a compressed crowd, lying packed like herrings in a barrel, the bumping against the sides of the locks, and the hissing of water therein like an inundation, startling one from sleep,—these things are very disagreeable. We suffered under an additional annoyance in the presence of sixteen presbyterian clergymen,—some of the most unprepossessing of their class. If there be a duty more obvious than another on board a canal-boat, it is to walk on the bank occasionally in fair weather, or at least to remain outside, in order

to air the cabin, (close enough at best,) and get rid
of the scents of the table before the unhappy passengers are shut up to sleep there. These sixteen
gentlemen, on their way to a Convention at Utica,
could not wait till they got there to begin their devotional observances, but obtruded them upon the
passengers in a most unjustifiable manner. They
were not satisfied with saying an almost interminable
grace before and after each meal, but shut up the
cabin for prayers before dinner ; for missionary conversation in the afternoon, and for scripture reading
and prayers quite late into the night, keeping tired
travellers from their rest, and every one from his fair
allowance of fresh air.

The passengers were all invited to listen to, and
to question a missionary from China, who was of the
party. The gentleman did not seem to have profited
much by his travels, however ; for he declared himself unable to answer some very simple inquiries.
" Is the religion of the Christian missionaries tole-
rated by the Chinese government?" " I am not
prepared to answer that question." " Are the Chinese cannibals?" " I am not prepared to answer
that question." One requested that any brother
would offer a suggestion as to how Government might
be awakened to the sinfulness of permitting Sunday
mails ; during the continuance of which practice there
was no hope of the Sabbath being duly sanctified.

No one was ready with a suggestion, but one offered a story, which every head was bent to hear. The story was of two sheep-drovers, one of whom feared God, and the other did not. The profane drover set out with his sheep, for a particular destination, two hours earlier than the other, and did not rest on Sunday like his pious comrade. What was the catastrophe? The God-fearing drover, though he had stood still all Sunday, arrived at his destination two hours earlier than the other. " Ah!" " Ah!" resounded through the cabin in all conceivable tones of conviction, no one asking particulars of what had happened on the road,—of how and where the profane drover had been delayed. Temperance was, of course, a great topic with these divines, and they fairly provoked ridicule upon it. One passenger told me that they were so strict that they would not drink water out of the Brandywine river : and another remarked that they partook with much relish of the strong wine sauce served with our puddings.

In addition to other discomforts, we passed the fine scenery of Little Falls in the night. I was not aware what we had missed till I traversed the Mohawk valley by a better conveyance, nearly two years afterwards. I have described this valley in my other work on America,* and must therefore restrain my pen from dwelling on its beauties here.

* " Society in America," vol. ii., p. 188.

The appearance of the berths in the ladies' cabin was so repulsive, that we were seriously contemplating sitting out all night, when it began to rain so as to leave us no choice. I was out early in the misty morning, however; and was presently joined by the rest of my party, all looking eagerly for signs of Utica being near.

By eight o'clock we were at the wharf. We thought Utica the most extempore place we had yet seen. The *right-up* shops, the daubed houses, the streets running into the woods, all seemed to betoken that the place had sprung up out of some sudden need. How much more ancient and respectable did it seem after my return from the west, where I had seen towns so much newer still! We were civilly received and accommodated at Bagg's hotel, where we knew how to value cold water, spacious rooms and retirement, after the annoyances of the boat.

Our baggage-master was fortunate in securing a neat, clean stage to take us to Trenton Falls (14 miles), where we promised each other to spend the whole day, on condition of being off by five the next morning, in order to accomplish the distance to Syracuse in the course of the day. The reason for our economy of time was not merely that it was late in the season, and every day which kept us from the Falls of Niagara, therefore, of consequence; but that our German friend, Mr. O., was obliged to be back in New York by a certain day. We all considered a little extra haste and fatigue a small tax to pay for the privilege of his companionship.

We clapped our hands at the sight of the " Rural Retreat," the comfortable, hospitable house of entertainment at Trenton,—standing in its garden on the edge of the forest,—so unlike hotels on the high road.

As no other company was there, we could choose our own hours. We ordered a late dinner, and proceeded to the Falls. We had only to follow a path in the pine forest for a few paces, and we were at the edge of the ravine which encloses the cascades.

It is a pity that the Indian name is not retained. Trenton Falls are called Cayoharic by the Indians. They are occasioned by the descent of West Canada Creek through a ravine, where it makes a succession of leaps from platforms of rock; six of these falls being pretty easily accessible by travellers. Much has been said of the danger of the enterprise of ascending the ravine; but I saw no peril to persons who are neither rash nor nervous. The two accidents which have happened have, I believe, been owing, the one to extreme rashness, and the other to sudden terror.

From the edge of the ravine, the black water, speckled with white foam, is seen rushing below with a swiftness which already half turns the head of the stranger. We descended five flights of wooden

steps, fixed against the steep face of the rock, and
at the bottom found ourselves at the brink of the
torrent.   I never was in so dark and chill a place in
the open air : yet the sun was shining on the opposite face of the rock, lighting the one scarlet maple
which stood out from among the black cedars and
dark green elms.   We selected our footing with a
care which we were quite ready to ridicule when we
came back ; and were not above grasping the chain
which is rivetted into the rock where the shelf which
forms the pathway is narrowest, and where the angles
are sharpest.   The hollow is here so filled with the
voice of many waters, that no other can be heard ;
and after many irreverent shouts had been attempted,
we gave up all attempts to converse till we reached
a quieter place.   Being impatient to see the first
fall, I went on before the rest, and having climbed
the flight of wooden steps, so wetted with the spray
of the fall as to be as slippery as ice, I stood on the
platform under a covert of rock foaming with the
thunder of the waters, and saw my companions, one
by one, turn the angle of the path, and pause in
front of the sheet of liquid amber, sprinkled with
snow.   The path on which they stood seemed too
narrow for human foot; and when, discerning me,
they waved their hands, I trembled lest, disregarding
their footing, they should be swept away by the
furious torrent.   When we found our heads turning

with the rush of the dark waters, we amused ourselves with admiring the little wells in the rock, and the drip from the roots of a cedar projecting from the top of the ravine,—a never-failing, glittering shower. Between the fifth and sixth fall there is a long tranquil reach of water; and here we lingered to rest our bewildered senses, before entering upon the confusion of rocks through which the sixth forces its way. We see-sawed upon a fallen trunk, sent autumn leaves whirling down the stream, and watched the endless dance of the balls of foam which had found their way into the tiny creeks and bays opposite, and could not get out again.

Gay butterflies seemed quite at home in this ravine. They flit through the very spray of the Falls. It seemed wonderful that an insect could retain its frail life in the midst of such an uproar. When the sun, in its course, suddenly shone full into the glen through a chasm in its rocky wall, how the cascade was instantly dressed in glory! crowned with a rainbow, and invested with all radiant hues! How the poor banished Indians must mourn when the lights of their Cayoharic visit their senses again in the dreams of memory or of sleep! The recollection of these poor exiles was an ever-present saddening thought in the midst of all the most beautiful scenes of the New World.

When we had surmounted the sixth fall, we saw

indeed that we could go no further. A round projection of rock, without trace of anything that I
could call a foot-hold, barred us out from the privacy of the upper ravine. The Falls there are said
to be as beautiful as any that we saw, and it is to
be hoped that, by blasting a pathway, or by some
other means, they also may be laid open to the
affections of happy visitors.

They have been seen and reported of. A friend
of mine has told me, since I was there, how Bryant,
the poet, and himself behaved like two thoughtless
boys in this place. Clambering about by themselves, one summer day, when their wives had gone
back to the house, they were irresistibly tempted to
pass the barrier, and see what lay beyond. They
got round the rock, I cannot conceive how, by ine-
qualities in its surface. They met with so many
difficulties and so much beauty higher up, that they
forgot all about time, till they found themselves in
utter darkness. They hastened to grope their way
homewards through the forest, and were startled,
after a while, by shouts and moving lights. Till
that moment, they never recollected how alarmed
their wives must be. It was past ten o'clock, and
the poor ladies had been in a state of uneasiness
half the evening, and of mortal terror for the two
last hours. They had got people from the neighbourhood to go out with torches, little expecting to

see their husbands come walking home on their own feet, and with nothing the matter with them but hunger and shame. I hope the ladies were exceedingly angry when their panic was over.

The forest at the top of the ravine was a study to me, who had yet seen but little forest. Moss cushioned all the roots of the trees; hibiscus overspread the ground: among the pine stems there was a tangle of unknown shrubs; and a brilliant bird, scarlet except its black wings, hovered about as if it had no fear of us. I could learn nothing more about it than that the people called it the red robin. Before we returned, the moon hung like a gem over the darkness of the ravine. I spent another happy day among these Falls, some months after, and was yet more impressed with their singularity and beauty.

When we had exchanged our wet clothes, an excellent dinner was served, and our host himself waited upon us, sitting down by the window when nothing was wanted. In the course of dinner, Mr. H. related to me some particulars of the slave insurrection at Charleston, a few years before, when upwards of thirty slaves were hanged at once. Some circumstance which he told led me to observe that I should have done as the thirty did, in their place. " Oh," said he, " so should " I thanked him for his response, saying that no defence he could now make of slavery would stand against such an admission. He did not retract, but a long argument ensued, in which our host became deeply interested. He moved his chair forwarder and forwarder, till I saw him leaning over the table between two of the gentlemen, to listen. Every body had long done eating, and every dish on the table was quite cold, and the debate concluded, before our host remembered that we had not had our pudding, and started up to serve us.

We soon retired to our rooms, being in need of rest after the discomforts of the canal-boat, and the fatigues of the day: but it was not too late for the neighbours to offer their hospitable welcomes. Just after I was undressed, the cards of visitors were brought me, with a friendly message: but it was too late to do more than send a message in return.

We left the place at a little after five in the morning, in a dismal rain. While breakfasting at Utica, we engaged an " exclusive extra " to carry us to Buffalo, for eighty dollars, the precise route being agreed upon, and the choice of times and seasons to remain with us. On going out to our carriage, we found the steps of the hotel occupied by a number of persons, some from Boston, who offered me welcome to the country, and any information or assistance I might need. One gentleman put into my hand a letter of introduction to an

influential friend of his at Cincinnati, as it was understood that I was going there. So from this
strange place, where I had not spent above two
hours, we drove off amidst a variety of friendly
greetings.

This day I first saw a log-house, and first felt
myself admitted into the sanctuary of the forest.
These things made the day full of interest to me,
though the rain scarcely ceased from morning till
night. Well settled farms were numerous along
the road; but in the intervals were miles of forest
—dark thronging trees with their soft gay summits.
Till now, the autumn woods had appeared at a distance too red and rusty; these, when looked into,
were the melting of all harmonious colours. As
for the forms, some were drooping, some towering,
their tall bare stems wreathed with crimson creep-
ers. The cleared hollows and slopes, with the forest
ever advancing or receding, are as fine to the imagination as any natural language can be. I looked
for an Indian or two, standing on the forest verge,
within a shade as dusky as himself; but for this I
had to wait another day.

Just after dark we arrived at Syracuse, in time
for the common supper. I was surprised at the
size and style of the hotel. Land and building material being cheap, and there being no window-tax,
there is little inducement to economize space in the

American houses; and the new hotels have the am-
bitious air which is given by spaciousness. The
deficiency lies in furniture, and yet more in attendance; but I really think that if travellers will trouble
themselves to learn a little of the ways of the house,
so as not to run into opposition to other people's
convenience, much more comfort may be enjoyed in
these places than unaccommodating tourists will believe. Our chambers were quite sufficiently furnished here; and I never, in any place, found difficulty in obtaining as large a supply of water as I
wished, by simply asking for it in good time. I
observed that the hotel parlours, in various parts of
the country, were papered with the old-fashioned
papers, I believe French, which represent a sort of
panorama, of a hunting party, a fleet, or some such
diversified scene. I saw many such a hunting
party, the ladies in scarlet riding-habits, as I remember the landlord of the inn at Bray, near Dub-
lin, to have been proud of in his best parlour. At
Schenectady, the bay of Naples, with its fishing-
boats on the water, and groups of lazzaroni on the
shore, adorned our parlour-walls. It seems to be
an irresistible temptation to idle visitors, English,
Irish, and American, to put speeches into the mouths
of the painted personages; and such hangings are
usually seen deformed with scribblings. The effect
is odd, in wild places, of seeing American witticisms

put into the mouths of Neapolitan fishermen, ancient English ladies of quality, or of tritons and dryads.

There is taste quite as bad as this in a matter of far more importance—the naming of places. Syracuse in the State of New York! I often wonder whether it is yet too late to revert to the Indian names,—to undo the mischief which has been done by boys, fresh from their smattering of the classics, who have gone into the forest to hew out towns and villages. I heard many Americans say that the State of New York ought to be called Ontario, and the city, Manhattan. But so far from bringing back the nomenclature to a better state, we not only find Utica, Syracuse, Manlius, and Camillus, and the village of Geneva on Seneca Lake, with Ithaca at its other extremity, but the village of Chittenango actually baptized into Sullivan: and all this in the neighbourhood of the lakes Onondago, Cayuga, and Owasco. It is as bad as the English in Van Diemen's Land, who, if I remember rightly, have got Palmyra, Richmond, and Jericho, all in a line.

Some curious associations arise from a new nation using the language of the old. While speculating sometimes on what the classical conceptions can be in the minds of youths who hear every day, in the most sordid connexion, of Rome, Utica, Carthage, Athens, Palmyra and Troy, it occurred to me that

some of our commonest English writing must bear
a different meaning to the Americans and to us.
All that is written about corn-fields, for instance,
must call up pictures in their minds quite unlike
any that the poets intended to create. " Waving
corn" is not the true description to them; and one
can scarcely bring one's tongue to explain that it
means " small grain." Their poetical attachments
are naturally and reasonably to their Indian corn,
which is a beautiful plant, worthy of all love and
celebration. But the consequence is that we have not
their sympathy about our sheaves, our harvest wain,
our gleaners; for though they have wheat, their
harvest, *par excellence*, is of corn cobs, and their
" small grain" bears about the same relation to
poetry with them as turnips with us.—Then, again,
there is the month of May, about which we lose their
sympathy. Over a great proportion of the country,
May is one of their worst months,—damp, drizzly,
with intervals of biting winds, as little fit for the
climate of a poem as our windy and dusty March.
Many other such particulars might be mentioned,
which it would be a new employment to trace out.

When I traversed New York State at a subsequent period with another party of friends, we saw
many Indians before reaching Syracuse. It was
at Oneida Castle, a village on the borders of the
Oneida territory, which was once fortified after the

Indian fashion; whence its formidable name. We saw in such close neighbourhood as to cause many strange reflections, the episcopalian church built for the Indians of the vicinity, who are declared to be reclaimed from idolatry, and their ancient Council Grove, where they met to think their own thoughts and say their own sayings. This grove is a fine clump of twenty-seven butter-nut trees. We passed through the village on the day when the Indians had all come in to receive their annual government allowance of seven dollars a head. Two men were drunk; the rest looked sober enough. The squaws were neatly dressed in blue pantaloons edged with white, and had clean blankets over their shoulders. The babies looked fat and lively. One squaw had her infant lashed to a board at her back. When we stopped to water the horses, we saw several boys with bows and arrows, and Dr. F. made them understand by signs that any one who could strike a quarter dollar which he would fix on a post, should have it. He made a notch in the post of a shed, and placed his coin, and forthwith the arrows flew like hail. One struck deep into a post, and we saw how easily fatal this weapon might be. An old Indian or two watched the sport, and assumed the superintendence. The coin fell, and Dr. F. was going to deliver it to the claimant, when an old Indian came forward with

" No, no."   He showed by signs that the coin had fallen, not from its being struck, but from the post having been shaken.   The quarter dollar was put up again, and soon after struck and bent in the middle by the arrow of a youth who looked as happy with his prize as if he had regained a tract of his native wood.   The party gave us some very bright looks as we drove away.

In a hotel on this road, I found a Sabbath School History of Lady Jane Grey, compiled obviously for the purpose of prejudicing the reader's mind against the catholics.   Among other wise things in it, there was an explanation that the heroine was called " Lady" because she was related to the king; and people are sometimes called so in England.   A clear idea to give the American youth of our English peerage !

We left Syracuse at dawn ; and this was the morning when, finding ourselves too hungry to proceed to Skaneatles without food, we were treated to that abundant breakfast, so characteristically served, which I have described in my other book.*   No one likes to breakfast twice over in description, any more than in reality; and I therefore say nothing about Elbridge here.—The greater part of this day, and some of the next, was spent at Auburn, in viewing the prison, walking about the town,

* " Society in America," vol. iii. p. 87.

and driving down the shores of the pretty Owasco Lake.

The cultivation of the country now began to show the improvement which increases all the way to Buffalo. At the head of Cayuga Lake, we travelled over the longest bridge I ever saw,—even a mile and eight rods long. It is wooden, of course, laid upon piles, and more conspicuous for usefulness than beauty. The great ornament of this route is the village of Geneva, reared on a terrace which overhangs Seneca Lake. The northern States abound in beautiful villages ; but I know none more captivating than this. A long row of handsome white and red houses, each with its sloping garden, fronts the lake ; and behind the dwellings, the road is bordered with locust trees, which seem to embower the place. The gardens are more carefully cultivated than is at all common in America, and they well repay the trouble bestowed on them. There is a college, standing on high ground above the lake, to which a natural lawn steeply descends from the open space in front of the building. Holstein, aide-de-camp to Bolivar, was professor of modern languages in this college when I was first at Geneva. Before my second visit he had removed to Albany. To crown the temptations of Geneva as a place of residence, it has a rather choice society. It has been charged with not being healthy; but I believe this is not true. It seems to be well and speedily supplied with literature. I saw a placard outside a bookseller's store, "Two Old Men's Tales, price 80 cents,"—that is, four shillings. One of my last interests, before I left England, had been watching over the publication of this work; and now here it was selling at four shillings, in the back of the State of New York! I remarked two things more about this village,— that all the women I saw were pretty, and that a profusion of azalea grew wild in the neighbourhood.

The road to Canandaigua ascends for a considerable distance, after leaving Geneva, and the last view of the place from above was exquisite, embosomed as it lay in the autumn woods, and with its blue lake stretched behind it in the sunny atmosphere. One element in the exhilaration of such scenes in America is the universal presence of competence. The boys who gather about the stage do not come to beg, or even to sell, but to amuse themselves while eating their bread and meat, or on their way to the field. The young women all well dressed, the men all at work or amusement, the farms all held in fee-simple, the stores all inadequate to their custom,—these things are indescribably cheering to witness, and a never-failing source of pleasure to the traveller from Europe. It may be a questionable comfort, but it *is* a comfort to think "if these people are not happy, it is their own fault." Whether their minds are as easy as their fortunes, it may not be safe to affirm; but at least the sin and sorrow of social injustice in regard to the first necessities of life are absent.

The moon was gleaming over Canandaigua Lake when we came in sight of it; and a golden planet dropped beneath the horizon when we took the turn towards the village. We found that Blossom's hotel did not answer to the favourable description which had been given us of it. This had been a training day, and the house was so noisy with drunken soldiers that when we had attained the drawing-room, we locked ourselves in till the house should be cleared, which happened as early as nine o'clock: but we still found the inn less comfortable than most upon the road.

The pretty village of Canandaigua is noted for its good society. It would have given me pleasure to have been able to accept the kind invitation of some of its inhabitants to prolong my stay now, or to revisit it the next year. But we had promised Mr. O. to cause no delay in getting to Niagara, and we engaged, in return for his agreeing to stop this day, to travel all night; and I never was able to allot any future time to this place. We saw as much of it, however, as we could in one day.

There are many families of Scotch extraction at

Canandaigua, and to this the village owes its superiority in gardens to almost any place in the country.
We spent the greater part of the day with a gentleman who was born in Scotland, but had settled at
Canandaigua thirty-four years before, when the
place was almost a desert. He now sees himself
surrounded by handsome dwellings, trim gardens,
and a highly-cultivated society, able to command
resources of books and other intellectual luxuries,
to almost any extent, from the directness and ease
of communication with New York. He had just
taken possession of a splendid new dwelling, and
had presented his old one to the episcopalian church
for a parsonage. He showed me, from the top of
the house, where this dwelling had stood, where it
stood now, and how it had been moved entire in a
day and a half. I think the distance could not have
been much under a mile.

After our early breakfast we were engaged till
church time in receiving and making calls, as there
was no time to be lost. We went to the episcopalian church with our friends, and heard a sermon
which could not please us,—it was so full of dog-
matism and bitterness. Our friends insisted on
entertaining the whole of our large party, and
invited some agreeable guests in addition, so that
we spent a very profitable as well as pleasant afternoon. We walked over the grounds, enjoyed the

view of the lake from the house-top, and picked up a good deal of information about the place and neighbourhood, which might seem to the inhabitants scarcely worthy of the name of knowledge, but which is inestimable to the stranger as opening new departments of enquiry, and explaining much which he did not understand before.

The stage was ordered for nine, and we returned to Blossom's for an hour's rest before setting out on our rough night's journey.

We reached Batavia to breakfast, and soon after found ourselves on the first piece of corduroy road we had encountered in the country.   I mention this because corduroy roads appear to have made a deep impression on the imaginations of the English, who seem to suppose that American roads are all corduroy.   I can assure them that there is a large variety in American roads.   There are the excellent lime stone roads which stretch out in three directions from Nashville, Tennessee, and some like them in Kentucky, on which the tourist might sketch almost without difficulty while travelling at a rapid rate. There is quite another sort of limestone road in Virginia, in traversing which the stage is dragged up from shelf to shelf, some of the shelves sloping so as to throw the passengers on one another, on either side alternately.   Then there are the rich mud roads of Ohio, through whose deep red sloughs the stage goes slowly sousing after rain, and gently upsetting when the rut on the one or the other side proves to be of a greater depth than was anticipated.   Then there are the sandy roads of the pine-barrens, of an agreeable consistency after rain, but very heavy in dry weather.   Then there is the ridge road, running parallel with a part of Lake Ontario, and supposed to be the edge of what was once its basin.   The level terrace thus provided by Nature offered the foundation of an admirable road, one of the best in the States.   Lastly, there is the corduroy road, happily of rare occurrence, where, if the driver is merciful to his passengers, he drives them so as to give them the association of being on the way to a funeral,—their involuntary sobs on each jolt helping the resemblance ;—or, if he be in a hurry, he shakes them like pills in a pill box.   But the American drivers are a class of men marked by that merciful temper which naturally accompanies genius.   They are men who command admiration equally by their perfection in their art, their fertility of resource, and their patience with their passengers.   I was never upset in a stage but once during all my travels ; and the worse the roads were, the more I was amused at the variety of devices by which we got on, through difficulties which appeared insurmountable, and the more I was edified at the gentleness with which our drivers treated female fears and fretfulness.

By this time a solitary Indian might be frequently

seen standing on a heap of stones by the road-side, or sleeping under a fence. There is something which rivets the eye of the stranger in the grave gaze, the lank hair, the blanket-wrapped form of the savage, as he stands motionless. We were generally to be seen leaning out of every opening in the stage, as long as the figure remained in sight.

We issued from the corduroy road upon one on which we could easily have performed twelve miles an hour. Houses with porches of Ionic pillars began to be scattered by the road-side. We were obviously approaching Buffalo. Soon the lake was visible, and then we entered the long main street, and stopped at the entrance of the Eagle hotel.

FORT ERIE.

" That night a child might understand
The de'il had business on his hand."
Burns.

ON consulting a good map, a little promontory may
be seen jutting out into Lake Erie on the Canada
shore, nearly opposite to Black Rock. Perhaps
it may be marked Fort Erie, for there Fort Erie
stood.

A lady of Buffalo, who happens to be a good
walker, proposed that she and I should indulge in a
ramble to Fort Erie, one fine day, towards the end
of October. She showed me that she was provided
with stout boots, in case of our having to cross
swampy ground; and she said she believed we
might trust to getting some sort of a dinner on the
Canada side, and might therefore go unencumbered
with provisions.

We set out from Buffalo soon after breakfast,
and made our way over a waste, through brush,
over fences, along a natural terrace once planted
with guns, down to the ferry at Black Rock. On
the way I saw one of the less prepossessing abodes
of settlers, so frequently described;—its desolate

appearance on the verge of the wood; its untidy garden, and the cool, uncomfortable manners, and the lank hair, and pale, dingy countenance of its mistress. I also heard, during our walk, some things which make me think that Buffalo is as undesirable a place of residence as any in the free States. It is the rendezvous of all manner of persons; the passage through which fugitives pass from the States to Canada, from Canada to the States, and from Europe and the Eastern States into the wild West. Runaway slaves come here, and their owners follow in hopes of recapturing them. Indian traders, land-speculators, and poor emigrants come here, and the most debased Indians, the half-civilized, hang about the outskirts. No influence that the mass of respectable inhabitants can exert can neutralize the bad effects of a floating population like this; and the place is unavoidably a very vicious one. A sufficient proof of this is, that ladies cannot walk beyond the streets without the protection of a gentleman. Some excellent English ladies opened a school in Buffalo, and not being aware of the peculiarities of the place, followed, with their pupils, the English practice of taking country walks. They persevered for some time, hoping to obtain countenance for the wholesome practice, but were compelled, after a time, not only to give up walking, but to quit the place.

It will be understood that I do not give this as any specimen of American towns. The corruption of Buffalo is owing chiefly to its frontier position, and consequent liability to a vicious, transient population.

After crossing the ferry at Black Rock, we pursued our walk in a south-west direction, sometimes treading a firm sand, and sometimes a greensward, washed by the fresh waters of the lake. Though we were on British ground, we were entertained by an American woman who lived on the lake shore, close by the fort. She treated us with negus and cake while preparing to get a dinner for us, and amused us with accounts of how butter and eggs are smuggled into Buffalo from her neighbourhood, these articles not being allowed to pass the Custom House. My eyes never rested on the Canada shore without my feeling how absurd it was that that poor country should belong to us, its poverty and hopeless inactivity contrasting, so much to our disgrace, with the prosperous activity of the opposite shore : but here was the climax of absurdity,—the prohibition of a free traffic in butter and eggs! What a worthy subject of contention between two great nations,—the one breaking the laws to provide Buffalo with butter and eggs, and the preventive force of the other exercised in opposition!

Our hostess was sewing when we went in, amusing

herself meanwhile with snatches of reading from " Peter Parley," which lay open before her. She put away her work to cook for us, conversing all the while, and by no means sorry, I fancy, to have the amusement of a little company. She gave us tea, beef-steak, hot rolls and butter, honeycomb, and preserved plums and crab-apples. Immediately after dinner I went out to the fort, my friend promising to follow.

The thickness of the remaining fragments of the walls shows the fort to have been substantially built. It was held by the Americans to the last extremity, in the war of 1814, and then blown up by a brave man to prevent its falling into the hands of the British. He remained alone in the fort to do the deed; and as I now witnessed the desolation of the solitude in which it stands, I felt as if I could enter into what his feelings must have been on the last day of his life. At one moment, all had been dead silence; at the next, the windows in Buffalo were blown out by the explosion.

I sat alone beside a pool in the middle of the fort. Fragments of the building lay tumbled around, overgrown with tall grass, and bristling with shrubbery. Behind me was the grim forest, with the ruins of a single deserted house standing within its shadow. Before me lay the waste of waters, with gulls dipping and sailing. A single birch overhung the pool beside me, and a solitary snipe, which seemed to have no fear of me, vibrated on the top of a bulrush. I do not know that I was ever so oppressed with a sense of solitude; and I was really glad soon to see my friend standing on a pinnacle of the ruined wall, and beckoning me to come up.

This afternoon, she told me her wonderful story; a part of which,—that part in which the public may be said to have an interest,—I am going to relate.

At the time of the war of 1812, Mrs. W. lived in Buffalo, with her father, mother, brothers, and sisters. In 1814, just when the war was becoming terrific on the frontier, her father and eldest brother were drowned in crossing the neighbouring ferry. Six months after this accident, the danger of Buffalo was so great that the younger children of the family were sent away into the country with their married sister, under the charge of their brother-in-law, who was to return with his wagon for the mother and two daughters who were left behind, and for the clothes of the family. For three weeks there had been so strong an apprehension of a descent of the Indians, the barbarous allies of the British, that the ladies had snatched sleep with their clothes on, one watching while the others lay down. It was with some difficulty, and after many delays, that the

wagon party got away, and there were still doubts
whether it was the safer course to go or stay. Nothing was heard of them before night, however, and
it was hoped that they were safe, and that the
wagon would come for the remaining three the
next morning.

The ladies put out their lights early, as they were
desired; and at eight, two of the three lay down to
sleep; Mrs. W., then a girl of sixteen, being one.
At nine, she was called up by the beating of a
drum, the signal that the Indians were at hand.
No description can give an idea of the loathing with
which these savages were then regarded,—the mingled horror, disgust, dread and hatred. The Indians were insidious, dangerous, and cruel beyond
example, even in the history of savage warfare.
These poor ladies had been brought up to hate
them with a deadly hatred; they were surrounded
with persons burning with the injuries inflicted by
Indian revenge and barbarity; for weeks they had
lived in hourly dread of death by their hands; their
strength was worn, and their nerves shaken by the
long suspense; and now the hoarse drum woke
them up with news that the hour was come. A
deadly sickness overspread their hearts as they
started from their beds. They looked from their
windows, but could see nothing through the blank
darkness. They listened, but they knew that if the

streets had been quiet as death, the stealthy tread of
the savages would have been inaudible. There was
a bustle in the town. Was the fight beginning?
No. It was an express sent by the scouts to say
that it was a false alarm. The worn-out ladies
composed their spirits, and sank to sleep again. At
four, they were once more wakened by the horrid
drum, and now there was a mustering in the streets
which looked as if this were no false alarm. In the
same moment, the sister who was watching what
passed in the street, saw by torch-light the militia
part asunder and fly, and Mrs. W., who was looking through the back window, perceived in the un-
certain glimmer that a host of savages was leaping
the garden-fence,—leaping along the walks to the
house, like so many kangaroos,—but painted, and
flourishing their tomahawks. She cried out to her
mother and sister, and they attempted to fly; but
there was no time. Before they could open the
front door, the back windows came crashing in, and
the house was crowded with yelling savages. With
their tomahawks, they destroyed everything but the
ladies, who put on the most submissive air possible.
The trunks containing the clothing of the whole
family stood in the hall, ready to be carried away
when the wagon should arrive. These were split
to fragments by the tomahawk. These wretches
had actually met the wagon, with the rest of the

family, and turned it back; but the brother-in-law, watching his opportunity, wheeled off from the road when his savage guards were somehow engaged, and escaped.

The ladies were seized, and as Mrs. W. claimed protection, they were delivered into the charge of some squaws to be driven to the British camp. It was unpleasant enough the being goaded on through such a scene by savage women, as insolent as the men were cruel; but the ladies soon saw that this was the best thing that could have happened to them; for the town was burning in various directions, and soon no alternative would be left between being in the British camp and in the thick of the slaughter in the burning streets. The British officer did not wish to have his hands full of helpless female prisoners. He sent them home again with a guard of an ensign and a private, who had orders to prevent their house being burned. The ensign had much to do to fulfil his orders. He stood in the doorway, commanding, persuading, struggling, threatening; but he saved the house, which was, in two days, almost the only one left standing. The whole town was a mass of smoking ruins, in many places slaked with blood. Opposite the door lay the body of a woman who in her despair had drunk spirits, and then defied the savages. They toma-hawked her, in sight of the neighbours, and before her own door, and her body lay where it had fallen ; for there were none to bury the dead. Some of the inhabitants had barricaded themselves in the jail, which proved, it was said, too damp to burn: the rest who survived were dispersed in the woods.

Before the fire was quite burned out, the Indians were gone, and the inhabitants began to creep back into the town, cold and half dead with hunger. The ladies kept up a large fire (carefully darkening the windows), and cooked for the settlers, till they were too weary to stand, and one at a time lay down to sleep before the fire. Mrs. W. often during those dreary days used to fasten a blanket, Indian fashion, about her shoulders, and go out into the wintry night, to forage for food,—a strange employment for a young girl in the neighbourhood of a savage foe. She traced the hogs in the snow, and caught many fowls in the dark. On the third day, very early in the morning, six Buffalo men were enjoying a breakfast of her cooking, when the windows were again broken in, and the house once more full of savages. They had come back to burn and pillage all that was left. The six men fled, and, by a natural impulse, the girl with them. At some distance from the house, she looked behind her, and saw a savage leaping towards her, with his tomahawk already raised. She saw that the next instant it would be buried in her skull. She faced about, burst out a laughing, and held out both her hands to the savage. His countenance changed, first to perplexity ; but he swerved his weapon aside, laughed, and shook hands, but motioned her home-wards. She was full of remorse for having quitted her mother and sister. When she reached her door, the house was so crowded that she could nei-ther make her way in, nor learn anything of their fate. Under the persuasion that they lay murdered within, she flew to some British dragoons who were sitting on the ground at a considerable distance, watching the burning of the remainder of the town. They expressed their amazement that she should have made her way through the savages, and guarded her home, where they procured an entrance for her, so that she reached the arms of her patient and suf-fering mother and sister. That house was, at length, the only one left standing; and when we returned, Mrs. W. pointed it out to me.

The settlers remained for some time in the woods, stealing in to a midnight warming and supper at the lone abode of the widow and her daughters. The ladies had nothing left but this dwelling. Their property had been in houses which were burned, and their very clothes were gone. The settlers had, however, carried off their money with them safely into the woods. They paid the ladies for their hospitality, and afterwards for as much needle-

work as they could do; for every one was in want
of clothes.   By their industry these women raised
themselves to independence, which the widow lived
some tranquil years to enjoy.   The daughter who
told me the story is now the lady of a Judge.   She
never boasts of her bravery, and rarely refers to her
adventures in the war ; but preserves all her readi-
ness and strength of mind, and in the silence of her
own heart, or in the ear of a sympathizing friend,
gratefully contrasts the perils of her youth with the
milder discipline of her riper age.

NIAGARA.

"Look back!
Lo! where it comes like an eternity,
As if to sweep down all things in its track,
Charming the eye with dread!"

Byron.

IT is not my intention to describe what we saw at Niagara, so much as to relate what we did. To offer an idea of Niagara by writing of hues and dimensions is much like representing the kingdom of Heaven by images of jasper and topazes.

I visited the Falls twice : first in October, 1834, in company with the party with whom we traversed the State of New York, when we stayed nearly a week ; and again, with Dr. and Mrs. F. and other friends, in June, 1836, when we remained between two and three days. The first time, we approached the Falls from Buffalo ; the next, from Lewiston and Queenston.

I expected to be disappointed in the first sight of the Falls, and did not relish the idea of being questioned, on the first day, as to my "impressions." I therefore made a law, with the hearty agreement of the rest of the party, that no one should ask an opinion of the spectacle for twenty-four hours.

We stepped into the stage at Buffalo at half-past eight in the morning on the 14th of October. At Black Rock we got out to cross the ferry. We looked at the green rushing waters we were crossing, and wondered whether they or we should be at the Falls first. We had to wait some minutes for the stage, on the Canada side, and a comely English woman invited us into her kitchen to warm ourselves. She was washing, as well as cooking; and such a log was blazing under her boilers as no fire-place in England would hold. It looked like the entire trunk of a pine, somewhat shortened. I could not help often wishing that some of the shivering poor of London could have supplies of the fuel which lies rotting in the American woods.

The road is extremely bad, all the way from the ferry to the Falls, and the bridges the rudest of the rude. The few farms looked decaying, and ill-clad children offered us autumn fruit for sale. We saw nothing to flatter our national complacency; for truly the contrast with the other side of the river was mournful enough.—It was not till we had passed the inn with the sign of the " Chippewa Battle Ground" that we saw the spray from the Falls. I believe we might have seen it sooner if we had known where to look. " Is that it?" we all exclaimed. It appeared on the left hand side, whereas we had been looking to the right; and instead of its being suspended in the air, like a white cloud, as we had imagined, it curled vigorously up, like smoke from a cannon, or from a replenished fire. The winding of the road presently brought this round to our right hand. It seemed very near: the river too was smooth as oil. The beginning of the Welland canal was next pointed out to me; but it was not a moment to care for canals. Then the little Round Island, covered with wood, and surrounded by rapids, lay close at hand, in a recess of the Canada shore. Some of the rapids, of eight or ten feet descent, would be called falls elsewhere. They were glittering and foamy, with spaces of green water between. I caught a glimpse of a section of the cataract, but not any adequate view, before we were driven briskly up to the door of the hotel. We ran quickly from piazza to piazza, till we reached the crown of the roof, where there is a space railed in for the advantage of the gazer who desires to reach the highest point. I think the emotion of this moment was never renewed or equalled. The morning had been cloudy, with a very few wandering gleams. It was now a little after noon; the sky was clearing, and at this moment the sun lit up the Horseshoe Fall.—I am not going to describe it.—The most striking appearance was the slowness with which the shaded green waters rolled over the brink. This majestic oozing gives a true idea of the volume of the floods; but they no longer look like water.

We wandered through the wood, along Table Rock, and to the ferry. We sat down opposite to the American falls, finding them, the first day or two, more level to our comprehension than the Great Horseshoe Cataract: yet throughout, the beauty was far more impressive to me than the grandeur. One's imagination may heap up almost any degree of grandeur; but the subtle colouring of this scene, varying with every breath of wind, refining upon the softness of driven snow, and dimming all the gems of the mine, is wholly inconceivable. The woods on Goat Island were in their gaudiest autumn dress; yet, on looking up to them from the fall, they seemed one dust colour. This will not be believed; but it is true.

The little detached fall on the American side piqued my interest at once. It looks solitary in the midst of the crowd of waters, coming out of its privacy in the wood, to take its leap by itself.—In the afternoon, as I was standing on Table Rock, a rainbow started out from the precipice, a hundred feet below me, and curved upwards as if about to alight on my head. Other such apparitions seemed to have a similar understanding with the sun. They went and came, blushed and faded, the floods rolling on, on, till the human heart, overcharged with beauty, could bear no more.

We crossed the ferry in the afternoon. Our boat was tossed like a cork in the writhing waves. We soon found that, though driven hither and thither by the currents, the ferryman always conquers at last, and shoots his boat into the desired creek : but the tossing and whirling, amidst the driving spray, seems a rather dubious affair at first. To be carried down would be no better than to be sucked up the river, as there is a fatal whirlpool below, which forbids all navigation as peremptorily as the Falls.

I still think the finest single impression of all is half-way up the American Fall, seen, not from the staircase, but from the bank, on the very verge of the sheet. Here we stood, this first evening, and amidst the rapids above. In returning, we saw from the river the singular effect of the clouds of spray being in shadow, and the descending floods in light; while the evening star hung over one extremity of the Falls, and the moon over the other, and the little perpetual cloud, amber in the last rays from the west, spread its fine drizzle, like a silver veil, over the scene.

There is nothing like patient waiting in a place like this. The gazer, who sits for hours watching what sun and wind may be pleased to reveal, is sure to be rewarded, somewhat as Newton described himself as being, when he set a thought before him, and sat still to see what would come out of it. It is surprising what secrets of the thunder cavern were disclosed to me during a few days of still watching,—disclosed by a puff of wind clearing the spray for an instant, or by the lightest touch of a sunbeam. The sound of the waters is lulling, even on the very brink; but if one wishes for stillness, there is the forest all around, where the eyes may become accustomed to common objects again. It is pleasant, after the high excitement, to stroll in the wild woods, and wonder what this new tree is and what that; and to gossip with the pigs, slim and spruce while fed on forest nuts and roots; and to watch the progress of a loghouse, sitting the while on a stump, or leaning over a snake-fence; and then to return, with new wonder, to the ethereal vision.

The first evening, the gentlemen were all restless under the prohibition to ask about impressions: every one of them was eager to tell, but too proud to pour out till others did the same. What an out-pouring it was when it did happen!

One morning, we found an old man, between seventy and eighty years old, gazing from Table Rock. He was an American. Being on a journey, he had walked from Queenston to see the Falls. He quietly observed that he was ashamed to think there had been wars near such a place, and that he hoped the English and Americans were grown wiser now, and would not think of fighting any more. This came in echo of my thought. I had been secretly wishing that all the enemies in the world could be brought together on this rock : they could not but love as brethren.

An English family at the hotel seemed marvellously skilled in putting away all the good influences of the place. The gentleman was so anxious about where he should settle, so incessantly pettish, so resolutely miserable, as to bespeak the compassion of all the guests for the ladies of his family, one of whom told me that she had forgotten all about the Falls in her domestic anxieties. As this gentleman found fault with every body and every thing, and ostentatiously proved that nothing could give him any pleasure, it was not surprising that the cataract itself failed to meet his approbation : yet I was not prepared for the question he put to me across the table, in the presence of both Canadians and Americans, whether I did not think the natives made a very silly fuss about the Falls, and whether the Falls of the Clyde were not much finer. Such are the persons by whom foreigners suppose themselves made acquainted with the English character. Such is the way in which not a few English study to mortify the inhabitants, and then come home and complain of American conceit. I told this gentleman that I perceived he was speaking of the rapids, and had not seen the Falls.

We wished, while we were in the neighbourhood, to obtain a glimpse of Lake Ontario, as we were not sure of being able to visit Canada at a future time.   We took the opportunity of two of our party going northwards, to accompany them as far as Queenston,—seven miles off,—where we intended to see Brock's monument, satisfy ourselves with the view from the top of it, and walk home through the woods in the afternoon.   In the stage were an Irish gentleman and his wife.   The lady amused me by the zeal with which she knitted all the way, just as if she were in a dark parlour in the Old Jewry ; and the gentleman with some sentiments which were wholly new to me ; for instance, he feared that the independence of the Americans made them feel themselves independent of God. This consequence of democratic government had not struck me before, and I never perceived any traces of its existence ; but if it should occur, there will probably soon be an epidemic or a bad season to bring them to their senses again.

Before the door of the wretched, foul inn at Queenston, we sorrowfully shook hands with our Prussian and Dutch companions, hoping to meet them again in the course of our travels ; which indeed happened more than once.—We provided

ourselves here with cider, cakes, and sandwiches;
i. e. beef-steak laid between thick dry bread. With
this provision, we ascended the hill to the foot of
Brock's monument, and found the portress, an
active little Irishwoman, waiting to let us in. She
was delighted to meet ladies from the old country,
and heartily invited us to spread our dinner in her
cottage below. She told us all her affairs, and
seemed unwilling to leave us when we told her we
meant to stay a long while on the top of the monument, and would not detain her from her wash-tub,
but would come down to her by-and-bye. She
and her husband have, for showing the monument,
sixty dollars a season, (that is, while the boats run,)
and all that they happen to take in the winter.
They were soon to have a cottage built for them
nearer the monument.—When we went down to
her cottage, she had spread plates, knives, and
pickles, and had her head full of questions and
communications. She was grateful for a small
payment for her trouble, and gave us the impression
of her being a very amiable, contented person, whom
we should like to see again.

Sir Isaac Brock fell at the battle of Queenston,
in October, 1812, near the base of this monument.
It is 145 feet high, and being built on a pretty
steep hill, commands a fine view. To the left a
prodigious sweep of forest terminates in blue Ca-

nadian hills.   On the right is the American shore,
at this time gaudy with autumn woods.   There
stands the village of Lewiston, with its winding
descent to the ferry.   At our feet lay Queenston,
its sordidness being lost in distance, and its long
street presenting the appearance of an English village.   The green river rushes between its lofty
wooded banks, which suddenly widen at Queenston,
causing the waters to spread and relax their speed,
while making their way, with three or four bends,
to the lake.   We saw the white church of Niagara,
rising above the woods, some miles off, where the
junction takes place; and beyond, the vast lake
spreads its waters, grey on the horizon.   There
was life in this magnificent scene.   The ferry boat
was buffeted by the waves ; groups were in waiting
on either side the ferry ; and teams were in the
fields.   The Irishwoman was grieved that she had
no telescope wherewith to enable us to see what
was doing on the lake.   She and her husband had
provided one for the accommodation of visitors.
Some travellers (English) had thrown it down from
the top of the monument, and when she asked for
payment, only bullied her ; and her husband had
not been able to afford to get another.

After dinner we sat on the top of the precipitous
wooded bank of the river, looking down into its
green eddies, and watching the family of white

birds which hovered far beneath us, but yet high
over the stream. Meditating as we were, that we
were now sitting on the spot where the Falls were
pouring down their floods ages before Babylon was
founded, or the Greek Mythology had arisen out of
the elements of universal conviction, it was not surprising that we had no thoughts to spare for the
weather *. We did not observe how the sky had
been darkening. Two wagons driven by lads
stopped in passing, and their drivers offered us
seats to Niagara. We at first declined, being bent
upon walking; but feeling heavy drops of rain at
the moment, we retracted our refusal, and jumped
into one of the vehicles. It was a mere box upon
wheels—a barbarous machine, but of great service
to us in the ensuing storm. Before we reached our
hotel we were thoroughly wet, but had obtained a
good deal of information from our driver about the
condition of the Canadian settlers in the neighbourhood. He was the son of a Canadian father and

---

* It is familiar to all that the cataract of Niagara is supposed
to have worn its way back from the point of the narrowing of its
channel (the spot where we now sat), and that there is an anticipation of its continuing to retire the remaining twelve miles to
Lake Erie. Unless counteracting agencies should meantime have
been at work, the inundation of the level country which must then
take place will be almost boundless. The period is, however, too
remote for calculation. An American told me, smiling, that the
apprehension has not yet affected the title to land. And no
one knows what secret barriers may be building up, or drains
opening.

Scotch mother, who were doing well in the world; as he said the English settlers do who set the right way to work. The land is not the best near the road; so that what is seen there is no fair specimen of the state of the settlers. The farms hereabout consist of about 100 acres generally, and are all the property of the residents. Labourers live with the farmers, and receive, besides their board and lodging, about 120 dollars a-year. A gentleman, a farmer and physician, from some distance, called on me one day when I was out, and left messages for me with one of our party. He said he wished me to see and do justice to Canada. People go, he believes, with wrong expectations, and so are disappointed. He, his wife and daughters, went, expecting ease and comfort, and they have found it; but they have not wealth and luxury. He declared that civility and cheerfulness would always command good manners and service. As I had no opportunity of " seeing and doing justice to Canada," I give this gentleman's testimony. It is very agreeable, and I do not doubt its justness.

Another visitor, of a very different kind, came to our parlour as I was preparing for our departure. I looked up from my packing, and saw an extraordinary apparition in the doorway;—a lady bridling, winking, and attitudinizing in a wonderful manner. On my asking her to come in and sit down, she said she was deputed by a gentleman to ask my address, in order to his communicating with me before I should publish my account of the Falls. She seemed deeply grieved at finding that I did not contemplate any such publication, saying that it would be a serious disappointment to the gentleman, who hoped I might have been of essential service to him—by recommending his hotel! It appeared that a sharp competition was going on about the letting of this hotel, and the gentleman in question was in hopes of getting it. He seemed to have one great qualification—the determination to leave no stone unturned.

The second time I visited Niagara, I accomplished the feat of going behind the Fall. In October it was too cold: on a sunny 8th of June there was no imprudence in it. When I descended the staircase with Dr. and Mrs. F., after breakfast, we had no such intention; but we were all tempted farther and farther over the rocks, nearer and nearer to the sheet, till the puffing away of the spray gave us glimpses of what was behind, and made us feel that this was the right day and hour. Mrs. F.'s chest was not very strong, and this was no enterprise for a child; so Dr. F. and I were to be the favoured ones. We ascended to the guide's house, and surveyed the extraordinary costume in which we were to make the expedition. Stout socks and shoes (but I would recommend ladies to go shod as usual), thick cotton garments reaching to the feet; green oilskin jackets and hats;—in this mountaineer sort of costume is the adventure to be gone through. As the guide's wife was assisting me, she hoped I had enjoyed myself since I was last at the Falls.

"Were you aware that I had been here before?"

"Yes, madam, I remember you well."

"Why, how is it possible that you should remember me among the thousands of people who have been here in two seasons? We were not acquainted, were we?"

"No, madam; but one evening you stopped and admired my cow."

"Did not this trumpet help you to remember me?"

"No, madam; I never saw it before."

How many ways there are to people's hearts! I now remembered having remarked to a companion on the beauty and docility of a cow which a woman was milking. The good wife had treasured up my observation as a personal compliment.

Mrs. F. and Charley accompanied us to the edge of the spray, when we sent them back, charging them not to expect us too soon, as we meant to look about us awhile.

We had a stout negro for a guide. He took me by the hand, and led me through the spray. I presently found the method of keeping myself at my ease. It was to hold down the brim of my hat, so as to protect my eyes from the dashing water, and to keep my mouth shut. With these precautions, I could breathe and see freely in the midst of a tumult which would otherwise be enough to extinguish one's being. A hurricane blows up from the cauldron; a deluge drives at you from all parts; and the noise of both wind and waters, reverberated from the cavern, is inconceivable. Our path was sometimes a wet ledge of rock, just broad enough to allow one person at a time to creep along: in other places we walked over heaps of fragments, both slippery and unstable.* If all had been dry and quiet, I might probably have thought this path above the boiling basin dangerous, and have trembled to pass it; but amidst the hubbub of gusts and floods, it appeared so firm a footing, that I had no fear of slipping into the cauldron. From the moment that I perceived that we were actually behind the cataract, and not in a mere cloud of spray, the enjoyment was intense. I not only saw the watery curtain before me like tempest-driven snow, but by momentary glances could see the crystal roof of this most wonderful of Nature's palaces. The precise point where the flood quitted the rock was marked by a gush of silvery light, which of

* A rope has since been stretched along the rock to serve for a hand rail. This must render the expedition far less formidable than before.

course was brighter where the waters were shooting forward than below, where they fell perpendicularly. There was light enough to see one another's features by, and even to give a shadow to the side of the projecting rock which barred our farther progress. When we came within a few paces of this projection, our guide, by a motion of his hand (for speaking was out of the question), forbade my advancing further. But it was no time and place to be stopped by anything but impossibilities. I saw that though there was no regular path on the other side of the guide, there were two pieces of rock, wide enough for my feet, by standing on which I might touch the wall which limited our walk. I made the guide press himself back against the rock, and crossed between him and the cauldron, and easily gained my object—laying my hand on Termination Rock. When I returned to my place, Dr. F. passed both the guide and myself for the same purpose. In returning, my hat blew off, in spite of all my efforts to hold it on. The guide put his upon my head, and that was carried away in like manner. I ought to have been instructed to tie it well on, for mere holding will not do in a hurricane. It is a proof that we were well lighted in our cavern, that we all saw the outline of a hat which was jammed between two stones some way beneath us. The guide made for this, looking just as if he were coolly walking down into destruction; for the volumes of spray curled thickly up, as if eager to swallow him. He grasped the hat, but found it too much beaten to pieces to be of any use.

Mrs. F. says we looked like three gliding ghosts when her anxious eye first caught our forms moving behind the cloud. She was glad enough to see us; for some one passing by had made her expect us at least two minutes before we appeared. Dripping at all points as we were, we scudded under the rocks, and up the staircase to our dressing-rooms, after which we wrote our names among those of the adventurers who have performed the same exploit, and received a certificate of our having visited Termination Rock. I was told that a fee and a wetting in the spray may secure such a certificate at anytime. Be this as it may, ours were honest.

When we came down in our own likeness, Mrs. F. had found a glorious seat for us on a rock which jutted outwards and upwards, commanding the entire range of the Falls, with every advantage of light, and also of solitude;—no inconsiderable gain in a place where tourists may be heard discussing on Table Rock the probability of there being chickens for dinner. I felt some pain in my chest for a few hours, but was not otherwise injured by the expedition. When the other members of our party joined us, they were somewhat surprised to hear what

we had done; and one of them followed our example another day.

I look back upon this morning as the very best
of the many I spent at the Falls. We found several new points of view, and the weather was divine.
We clambered down to the water's edge, where men
were gathering spars and other " curiosities." We
sat long amusing ourselves with watching the vain
attempts of the tree-trunks, which had been carried
over from above, to get any farther down the river.
They were whisked about like twigs in the boiling
waters, and sometimes made a vigorous shoot, as if
to get free of the eddies; but as often as they
reached a particular spot, they were sure to be
turned back, and sucked up the stream, to try
again. I think they must be doing penance there
still, unless, enormous logs as they are, they have
been dashed to pieces. When the sun became too
hot to be borne below, we came up to the foot of
the staircase, and sat in the shade, drinking from
the drip,—the soft shower which could not make
itself heard amidst the solemn roar of the floods.
Here Charley stood, placing spouts of reed which
might convey water from the drip, wherewith to
wash his spars. Not a word of wonder had we
from him. He gloried in the scene, and feared
nothing, climbing, with the help of his father's
strong hand, wherever it was practicable to set his

little foot : but there was no wonder. The age of wonder has not arrived to children, savages, and other ignorant persons. They know too little of purposes, means, and obstructions to be aware of what either divine or human achievement is. A child believes you if you promise to take him into the moon ; and a savage supposes that you eclipse the sun by firing a musket. An ignorant person annoys Mr. Babbage, after much praise of his machine, by asking to know one thing more,—" If you put a question in wrong, will the answer come out right?" Charley would hardly have asked this question, child as he was ; but he did not share our wonder at the cataract. He enjoyed the climbing, and the rainbows, and the emerald pillars based on clouds, which was the form the floods bore, this sultry noon ; but he went on washing his spars as tranquilly as if he had been beside our favourite brook in the wood at Stockbridge. His pity was stirred up this morning, however, with a story of a bird which I saw perish. It had got bewildered in the circuit of the Horse Shoe Fall. I saw it driving and fluttering about for a minute or two in the spray, when it flew directly into the sheet, and was swallowed up.

The next day was devoted to Goat Island. Dr. F., who learned English to the last degree of perfection in little more than two years, happened to say, one day, that there was one English word whose exact meaning he did not understand,—*dawdle*. We promised to afford him an exemplification of it this day. There was also a joke against me. I was now a practised traveller; and having found how the pleasures of travelling are economized by business-like habits of arrangement, I was the prompter of our somewhat inexperienced party about ordering dinner, packing at convenient times, and so contriving as to have our thoughts at perfect liberty for pleasure while we were out-of-doors, instead of having to run or send to our lodgings about business which might as well have been settled while we were there. They asked me whether I could spend a whole day without thinking of time, meals, or the fitness of things in any way. No one was better pleased with such liberty than I; so we left behind us even our watches. It appears, however, that somebody must have carried money, for food was brought to us, and doubtless honestly paid for.

At some unknown hour of a bright morning, therefore, we set forth from our hotel, and in due time reached the ferry. The entire party paid sufficient attention to business to sit properly in the boat, which is no place for freak and frolic, while bobbing about among the eddies. We *dawdled* long about the American Fall. I had never before been fully aware of its power over the senses. To-day, I saw a lady who was sitting on the bank,—as safe a seat as an arm-chair by the fireside,—convulsively turn away from the scene, and clasp the ground. Yet the water falls so tranquilly that I should not be afraid to stand in the flood, near the bank where it takes the leap. I tried the force of the water there, and found it very moderate. After completing the ascent, Mrs. F. and I were standing looking at the rapids, when a letter was handed to me. Somebody had actually been mundane enough to remember the post-office, and to go to it! I was glad it was not I. Further sins against the spirit of the day were presently committed. Of course, I cannot say what time it was, but, by the heat, probably about the middle of the day, when the ladies were sitting on the stem of a tree, in a tiny island, amidst the roaring rapids,—an interesting love-story being their topic,—and the gentlemen were seen approaching with bread, biscuits, cheese, ale, and lemonade. They had not even forgotten glasses. We ate our dinner on a bench under the trees,—all except Charley, who niched himself in an ash, which parted from the root into many stems. The boy looked like a beautiful fairy, and for his own part declared that this was far better than dining in any house.

We dawdled hours away in Goat Island; now lying on the grassy bank with our feet almost into the rapids; now fanning ourselves in the translucent green shades of the wood, among rabbits and goats, and then gathering new wild flowers from the multitude which blossomed under our feet; the roar of the Falls solemnizing all. The timid ones sat in the alcove erected above the Horse Shoe Fall, while the rest went down to the Terrapin Bridge and Tower. The tower, forty feet high, is built on rocks in the midst of the rapids, and its summit affords an absolutely complete view of the scene. The bridge is built on logs which extend from rock to rock in the rapids, to the edge of the precipice, the flood gushing beneath in a dizzying whirl. At my first visit, this bridge had been complete, and to all appearance secure. I had stood on its extreme point, which projected over the precipice. There I hung suspended above the fall,—standing in the air on the extremity of a beam, and without any suspicion that I was not perfectly safe. It was there that I learned some of the secrets of the cataract. I saw there what can be seen nowhere else, —the emerald columns broken and forced up, and falling again in gushes of diamonds, which again were melted into wreaths of dazzling snow. It was now too late to see this any more. The bridge had broken down, some way from the end; the handrail was gone, and the brink of the precipice was no longer accessible. We got to the tower, however, and further; and Charley and his father stepped down from the bridge among the rocks, and stood amidst the water, very near the brink of the great Fall! Their position was shown to be perfectly safe by the verdure of these rocks. Slight shrubs, rooted in their crevices, were full of leaf. Their smallest twigs were tossed in the never-dying breeze, without being snapped. Yet we were glad when our friends were safe on the bridge again.

We descended the Biddle staircase,—the spiral staircase fixed against the perpendicular rock in Goat Island,—and pursued a narrow path from its foot back to the Fall, where we found a glacier! An enormous pile of snow and ice lay against the rock, so solid, under this intense June sun, that Charley climbed to the top of it. Here every successive pulse of the cataract was like a cannon shot a few yards off; so that there was no standing it long; there was much yet to do; and the party probably observed, though no one chose to mention it, that the sun was going down. We crossed the detached American Fall, by its rustic bridge, and hunted it back to its retreat in the wood. Our faces were now turned homewards; but we lingered long in the shades, and afterwards at Bath Island, where some one observed that it would be dusk before we could reach the ferry, and that the walk home on the Canada side was not of a kind to be prosecuted in the dark. The sun disappeared be-

fore we reached the ferry-house, and the panorama
from the river was seen in the magnitude and majesty of twilight.   In the dark woods on the Canada
side, we made ourselves visible to each other by
catching fire-flies and sticking them in our bonnets.
They sat very still among our bows of ribbon, and
really served our purpose very well.

Bad news awaited us at home,—news of Mr.
Van Buren's casting vote in favour of the third
reading of the Gag Bill; and of a fresh breaking
out of the dreadful Creek war in Georgia: but now
that that atrocious bill has long been thrown out,
and the Creek war ended, (though with grievous
suffering and humiliation to the poor Creeks,) this
day of delicious dawdling (a word which Dr. F.
by this time completely understood,) stands out
bright enough to be worthy of the scene and of our
human life.

PRIESTLEY.

"Ingrata Patria !"

Dante's Epitaph.

" Que l'homme donc s'estime son prix :—il a en lui la capacité
de connôitre la vérité, et d'être heureux : mais il n'a point de
vérité, ou constante, ou satisfaisante. Je voudrois donc porter
l'homme à désirer d'en trouver ; à être prêt et dégagé des passions
pour la suivre où il la trouvera."—*Pascal.*

AMONG the select classes of men to whom the
common race looks up with the heart-throb of
mingled reverence and sympathy, none is perhaps
so eminent as that of sufferers for opinion. If ever
we are conscious of a breathing of the God-head in
man, it is in the sanctified presence, actual or ideal,
of martyrs to truth. Such men, as a class, are
liable to particular faults, are usually marked by
the imperfections which attend their virtues, as shadows are a consequence of sunshine. But in no
case are men in general so tolerant of faults as in
theirs ;—I do not mean in their own day, when they
are not commonly recognised as confessors and martyrs,—but when they stand out from the records of
time, complete characters in history. The turbulence, jealousy, and self-will of such men are

allowed for more liberally than the same faults in other orders of men,—more slightly noticed,—more eagerly extenuated. And why? Because, of all men, they most infallibly and extensively command sympathy. As truth is the one eternal good, the single pursuit of truth is the one eternal virtue which wins and elevates all human souls.—But when, as in some rare instances, this devotion to truth is seen purified from the failings which elsewhere seem its natural accompaniments,—when the hero is seen holy, harmless, and undefiled as the sage,—when no regrets need mingle with the admiration of the disciple, as delicious a contemplation is afforded to the moral taste as the moral creation yields.

Such was Priestley, the single-minded martyr, but the meek inquirer; the intrepid confessor, but the humble Christian; the gentle philosopher, the sympathising friend. Circumstances have been unfavourable to a wide, but not to a full knowledge of his character. The comparatively few to whom his mind and heart have been absolutely laid open, regard him with a love which is only not idolatrous because it is perfectly reasonable. The many know him as a man who was driven away from Birmingham by a mob who destroyed his house, papers, and philosophical apparatus, burned his church, and sought his life; and that he took refuge in America, and died there. Some go on to believe what was said at the time—that he was a turbulent man, a mischief-maker, and either a conceited smatterer in theology and philosophy, or a deep malignant infidel,—they do not know which. Others hold him to have been a good kind of man, who rashly drew upon his own head the tempests of his time, and had to bear only the natural though hard consequences of his own imprudence. But those whose knowledge of him is complete can tell that his imputed turbulence was intellectual activity; his conceit a simplicity too lofty for the apprehension of his enemies; his infidelity a devout constancy to truth. His depth was all of wisdom : his hatreds were of cant, hypocrisy, and designed obstruction of truth. He exposed himself to tribulation as innocently and unconsciously as he bore it meekly and heroically. He never sought martyrdom, for he loved life and its comforts in the bosom of his family and friends ; he valued repose for his philosophical pursuits, and thought his daily probation sufficient for every man's strength. He was playing backgammon with his wife after supper when the mob came upon him : he was so wholly unprepared that his MSS. and private letters lay all exposed to the rioters ; and the philosopher suffered,—calmly and bravely suffered—the anguish of feeling himself a hated and an injured man. Yet, thus taken by surprise, his emotions were not for himself, or for the many near and dear friends who were being overwhelmed with him.   While he stood looking over a garden hedge where he could see the flames devouring his church, and hear the shouts of the mob which was demolishing his house, he dropped a natural expression of pity for the misery of those poor people when they should discover what mischief they had done.   No word was ever heard from him about the effect which the sufferings of the day would have upon any body's mind, or upon any future time.   He simply did the duty, and bore the probation of the hour, leaving unconsciously an example of sublime patience which has raised and kindled more minds than the highest order of good men ever dream of influencing, and whose force will not be spent while men are moved by disinterestedness, or thrilled by heroism.

Of his retirement in America we have many particulars, but still not enough.   Enough can never be learned of the course of life of one whose more homely virtues were now put to the severest test, after those which are commonly esteemed more lofty had well stood their trial.   The following passage delivers over to us the impression of the philosopher's latter days, which Priestley's own correspondence, and the notices of his friends leave on the mind of an affectionate admirer of the man.

" There, in one of its remote recesses, on the outer margin of civilization, he, who had made a part of the world's briskest activity, who had led on the speed of its progress, whose mind had kept pace with its learning, and overtaken its science, and outstripped its freedom and its morality, gathered together his resources of philosophy and devotion; thence he looked forth on the vicissitudes and prospects of Europe, with melancholy, but hopeful interest, like the prophet from his mount, on the land whose glories he was not to see. But it was not for such an energetic spirit as his to pass instantaneously into the quietude of exile without an irrecoverable shock. He had not that dreamy and idle pietism which could enwrap itself in the mists of its own contemplations, and believe Heaven nearer in proportion as earth became less distinct. The shifting sights and busy murmurs that reached him from afar, reminded him of the circulation of social toils which had plied his hand and heart. Year after year passed on, and brought him no summons of duty back into the stir of men; all that he did he had to devise and execute by his own solitary energies, apart from advice and sympathy, and with no hope but that of benefitting the world he was soon to quit. The effort to exchange the habits of the city for those of the cloister was astonishingly successful. But his mind was never

the same again; it is impossible not to perceive a
decline of power, a tendency to garrulity of style
and eccentricity of speculation in his American
publications.   And yet, while this slight, though
perceptible shade fell over his intellect, a softened
light seemed to spread itself over his character.
His feelings, his moral perceptions, were mellowed
and ripened by years, and assumed a tenderness and
refinement not observable before.   Thanks to the
genial and heavenly clime which Christianity sheds
round the soul, the aged stem burst into blossom.
And so it will always be when the mind is really
pervaded by so noble a faith as Priestley's.   There
is no law of nature, there are no frosts of time, to
shed a snow-blight on the heart.   The feelings die
out when their objects come to an end; and if there
be no future, and the aims of life become shorter
and shorter, and its treasures drop off, and its attractions are spent, and a few links only of its hours
remain in the hand, well may there be no heart for
effort, and no eye for beauty, and well may love
gather itself up to die.   But open perfection to its
veneration, and immortality to its step; tell it of
one who is and always will be the inspirer of genius,
the originator of truth, the life of emotion; assure
it that all which is loved shall live for ever; that
that which is known shall enlarge for ever, that all
which is felt shall grow intenser for ever, and the

proximity of death will quicken instead of withering
the mind; the eye will grow dim on the open page
of knowledge; the hand will be found clasping in
death the instruments of human good; the heart's
last pulse will beat with some new emotion of
benignity.   In Priestley's case there was not merely
a sustainment, but a positive advancement of character in later years.   The symptoms of restlessness
gradually disappear without abatement of his activity; a quietude as of one who waits and listens
comes over him; there are touches of sentiment
and traces of tears in his letters, and yet an obvious
increase of serenity and hope; there is a disposition
to devise and accomplish more good for the world,
and ply himself while an energy remained, and yet
no anxiety to do what was beyond his powers.   He
successively followed to the grave a son and a wife;
and the more he was left alone, the more did he
learn to love to be alone; and in his study, surrounded by the books which had been his companions for half a century, and over half the earth,
and sitting beneath the pictures of friends under the
turf, he took his last survey of the world which had
given him so long a shelter: like a grateful guest
before his departure, he numbered up the bright
and social, or the adventurous hours which had
passed during his stay; and the philosophers who
had welcomed him in his annual visits to London,—

the broad, sagacious face of Franklin, the benignant intelligence of Price, rose up before him, and the social voices of the group of heretics round the fire-side of Essex Street, floated on his ear; and as the full moon shone upon his table, and glistened in his electrical machine, his eye would dream of the dining philosophers of the Lunar Society, and glisten to greet again the doughty features of Darwin, and the clear, calculating eye of Watt. Yet his retro-spective thoughts were but hints to suggest a train of prospective far more interesting. The scenes which he loved were in the past, but most of the objects which clothed them with associations of interest were already transferred to the future: there they were in reserve for him, to be recovered (to use his own favourite phrase, slightly tinged with the melancholy spirit of his solitude) 'under more favourable circumstances;' and thither, with all his attachment to the world, whose last cliffs he had reached, and whose boundary ocean already murmured beneath, he hoped soon to emigrate."*

Priestley had much to suffer in America. His severest woes befel him there. There he lost his beloved son Harry; then his wife departed; and trials which exceeded even these put his Christian acquiescence to the fullest proof. To an intimate

* " Monthly Repository," New Series, vol. vii., p. 235.

friend he writes—" From how much trouble has my wife been relieved ! She had a great mind, but the events that have taken place since her death would have affected her deeply. My trials, now towards the close of life, are as great as I can bear, though I doubt not that a wise and good Providence overrules all events, and I have daily a more habitual respect to it. Nothing else could support me. . . . We are frail, imperfect beings, and our faith is at best but weak, and requires to be strengthened by reading and reflection. I never omit reading, and I do it with more satisfaction than ever, a considerable portion of Scripture every day, and by this means my mind is much relieved."

This is not the device of the devotee, the refuge of the disappointed man who takes to religion as the only resource left him. This is the declaration of a philosopher, whose youth and whose riper years were given to the close study of the book which was now the pillow of his age.

I know not how it may appear to persons less familiarised than myself with the spirit of the man, and the eloquent moderation of his language, but I have always regarded the letter on the death of his son Harry as an exquisite revelation of a healthy mind in sorrow :—

" *Northumberland, Dec.* 17, 1795.

" Dear Friend,

" I think that in my last, of the 7th instant, I mentioned Harry's being indisposed; in consequence, we imagined, of his attending his limekiln in the night. It proved to be a more serious illness than we or the physician imagined. He grew worse till the 11th, when he died, it is now almost certain, of an inflammation and mortification of the stomach. Having had little or no apprehension of danger till near the time of his death, the shock, you may suppose, was very great; and being the first event of the kind, I am affected more than I thought I should have been, though I have unspeakable consolation in believing that nothing can befal us without the appointment of the best of Beings, and that we shall meet our departed children and friends in a better state.

" He had recovered from an ague, which was common in this part of the country, this summer; but after this, he had frequent colds, from exposing himself to cold and wet, and not taking proper care of himself afterwards, which certainly laid the foundation of his subsequent and last illness.

" Had he been bred a farmer, he could not have been more assiduous than he was. He was admired by every body for his unremitting labour, as well as good judgment, in the management of his business, though only eighteen years old. With respect to his ardour in his pursuits, he was more like what I was at his age than any of my children, though our objects were very different. He was strictly virtuous, and was uncommonly beloved by all that worked under him; and it was always said that he was better served than any other farmer in this country. He had a sense of honour and generosity which, I am sorry to say, is not common here. I hope, therefore, that he had the foundation of something in his character, on which a good superstructure may be raised hereafter. We thought his temper, and even his looks, altered for the worse by the severe illness he had at Hackney; but it is remarkable, that some time before his death, (as his mother, who never left him, says,) and very visibly afterwards, he had the same sweet, placid, and even cheerful countenance, that he had when he was young; much like that of his sister, whom, at that time, he greatly resembled. I never saw the countenance of a dead person so pleasing; and so it continued till he was buried. Even this seemingly trifling circumstance gives me much satisfaction. I know you and Mrs. Lindsey will excuse my writing so much about myself and family. I could not write so much to any body else.

*   *   *   *   *

" My wife is much affected, as you will suppose, by the death of Harry ; but, at the same time, discovers proper fortitude.   By her constant attendance upon him, she has made herself ill, but seems to be getting better."*

This is the man whom Johnson dared to execrate. At a chemical lecture, he knit his brows, and was displeased with the lecturer for citing so often the discoveries of Dr. Priestley.   When excuse was made that chemical lectures could not be faithfully given without citing Priestley's discoveries, " Well," said the moral Johnson, " I suppose we must give even the devil his due."   Thus may even great men revile greater, denouncing those to whom it would be well for them to kneel.

There are some who are as blind to Priestley's merits as Johnson, without half his excuse.   Before I went to America I was aware that the Unitarians there, who ought to know every thing about the apostle of their faith who took refuge in their country, were so far in the dark about him, as that they misapprehended his philosophy, and misrepresented its tendencies in a way and to a degree which seemed irreconcileable with the means of information within their reach.   I knew that Dr. Channing's celebrated note on Priestley

* Rutt's Life, Correspondence, and Works of Priestley, Vol. i. Part ii. p. 327.

remained unretracted,—though rebuked on the spot*
with much spirit and tenderness by a then young
divine, who better understood the Christian sage.
I knew that the tendency of this sect in America
to lean upon authority,—with some other causes,—
must indispose them to do justice to Priestley.
But till I was among them, I had no idea that it
was possible for those of them who were not ignorant of the character of the philosopher to allow
their fear and dislike of some of his convictions to
render them so insensible as they are to the majesty
of the man. They themselves would deny the
insensibility, and point to this and that testimony to
Priestley being a well-meaning man, which may be
found in their publications. But facts show what
the insensibility is. Dr. Channing speaks of him
now in a tone of patronage, admitting that he is
under obligations to him for one or two detached
sermons which breathe the true spirit. Another
clergyman puts forth a small volume of selec-
tions from Priestley's works, with an apologetical
preface, which states, that whatever Priestley's doctrines and writings may have been as a whole, there
are portions which may be picked out for people to
profit by. Such facts show that the character and
mission of the man are not understood. Priestley
was, above most men, one who came at a right

* In the " Christian Disciple."

point of time to accomplish a particular service; to
break up the reliance on authority in matters of
opinion and conscience, and insensibly to show, in
an age when prejudice and denial were at fierce
war, how noble and touching is the free and fervent
and disinterested pursuit of truth.   His character
is to everlasting; but his writings are, for the most
part, suitable to only a particular position of affairs,
a critical social state.   Those who, like the Americans, are unprepared for—alienated from—his
philosophy, and who are remarkable for their
dependence on authority in matters of opinion,
cannot possibly sympathise with Priestley's convictions; and a full appreciation of him ought not to
be expected of them.   But they had better, in such
a position of circumstances, let his works alone.   It
is not necessary or desirable that they should study
writings to which no impulse of sympathy or admiration leads them; but it is most desirable that
they should not speak and write apologetically and
patronisingly of one of the largest-minded and most
single-hearted of sages.   In the transition which
the religious and philosophical society of America
has to make, from reliance on authority to a state of
individual research and conviction, the philosopher
may or may not yet become an apostle to them.
In their present condition, he cannot be so.   The
warmest friends of both see that it cannot be so.
They only desire that his reputation should be left

unvisited as his remains; and that while no traveller is drawn aside from his path to seek the philosopher's tomb, no presumptuous hand should offer to endorse his merits, or push the claims to partial approbation of one who was created to command reverent discipleship; reverent discipleship in the pursuit of truth, if not in the reception of doctrine.

The first point of my travels fixed in my intentions was the retreat of Priestley; and my pilgrimage thither was accomplished within a few weeks after I landed. From Pittsburgh we crossed the Alleghanies by the road through Ebensburg, and in four days reached Youngmanstown, eighteen miles from Northumberland. We breakfasted at Lewisburg on the 11th of November, and were very glad to leave behind us the most fretful stage company we were shut up with in all our travels. We crossed the Susquehanna in peace and quiet, and could freely enjoy our meditations, as every mile brought us nearer the philosopher's resting-place. I wish I could communicate to others of his disciples the harmony between the scenery and the man which now exists, and ever will exist, in my own mind. Priestley himself wrote, " I do not think there can be, in any part of the world, a more delightful situation than this and the neighbourhood;" and I revolved this in my thoughts as I gazed upon the broad, shoaly, and gleamy river

bordered with pines, and the swelling hills and
sloping fields which sometimes intervened between
us and the river. The morning was one of lustrous
clouds and mild gleams; and the whole scene was
of the tranquil character, and dressed in the soft
light, which is most accordant with the mood of
those traversing the scenery with such reasons as
mine. I was full of stronger emotions than when
I found myself in sight of the spray of Niagara.
There is nothing so sanctifying as the ideal presence
of the pure in spirit; and not all the thronging
images of what Niagara had witnessed since the
earliest worship of an extinct race was paid there,
before the ancient empires of the earth were heard
of, affected me so much as the thought of the sage
who came hither to forgive his enemies, and hope
all things for the world, in the midst of his hourly
privations and daily regrets.

Abrupt wooded rocks dignify the river banks near
the town; and nothing can be much more beautiful than the situation of the place, in the fork of
the Susquehanna. The town itself, however, would
delight an improvement-hater. It has scarcely
advanced at all since Priestley's time. Some of
the inhabitants complain that this stagnation is
owing to the want of enterprise among their capi-
talists; but there would be enterprise there as
elsewhere, if there was an average prospect of

reward. Others allege that the place is not healthy. It is certainly subject to fever and ague; but the causes are thought to be removable. Sunbury, on the other shore of the eastern branch of the river, is a rival, a thriving competitor of Northumberland ; but the growth of neither is to be compared with that of most American towns. The only interest connected with Northumberland still is its being Priestley's city of refuge.

We were hospitably received at the clean little inn; and I presently discovered that our hostess could give me more information about Priestley than anybody else in the place. Her father had been intimately acquainted with the philosopher; had been his confidant in his latest and severest trials ; and she herself remembered him well, and could relate many little incidents which delighted me as giving life to objects that were before my eyes. No words can convey the passionate admiration, the devoted love with which this good lady spoke of him. A power went out of him which melted his enemies, and converted those who came with hatred into his presence; and it exalted the love of his friends to the highest pitch that human affection can reach. " All that I have formerly said of Dr. Priestley is nonsense," declared a stiff religious bigot, after an accidental interview with the philosopher. " I have now seen him for my-

self, and you must let me see more of him." Our
good hostess told me how unequalled his preaching
was, so simple and earnest and tender, quite unlike
any other person's preaching, and his looks so
bright : she dwelt on his goodness to his neighbours,
and told how inexhaustible were his charities,—so
thoughtful, so steady, so perpetual. She laughed
again at the remembrance of his child-like gaiety,
bursting out in the midst of his heart-soreness, and
declared that he was never long depressed : he was
so sure that all was right in reality, that he could
never be dismayed at its seeming otherwise for a
time. She remembered that " he was much thought
of when he first came," yet she never felt afraid of
him. She was present at the only time when he
was seen wholly overcome by grief, and will never
forget the oppression of heart, the anguish of seeing
tears streaming down his face when no one could do
anything to help him. But her recollections of
him are chiefly joyous,—of his eagerness about his
philosophical pursuits ; the cheerful tone of his
preaching ; his sympathy with young people. Never
was a lovelier picture of old age given,—of its virtues, nor, alas ! of its privileges,—than by this affectionate observer. Her testimony is confirmed by
every other that exists. I saw the gentleman who
was with him when he received his Voltaic pile, and
who told me how eagerly he pointed out the wire

dissolving, and made his friend take a shock in his
fore-finger.   All who conversed with him mentioned
that his feelings became more sensitive towards the
end of his life; his eyes were frequently seen to
glisten in conversation, and he smiled oftener.   A
gentleman, now well known as an unbeliever of the
last degree of bigotry, who shrinks with as much
hatred and fear from the very mention of religion
as persons of an opposite character from infidelity,
bore a singular testimony to the state of Priestley's
mind in his latter days.   This gentleman was observing to me that it was strange, considering how
irritable Priestley's temper was by nature, and that
he died of a harassing and depressing disease, that
he was eminently placid during the last few months
of his life.   I observed that his religion was of a
sustaining nature, being no superstition, but a firmly-
grounded, long-tried faith; and that the natural explanation of his tranquillity was that he was in a
thoroughly religious state of mind.   " Religious!
bless me, no!" cried the gentleman : " he was
always very cheerful whenever *I* saw him."

At the house of his grandson, cashier of the bank
at Northumberland, I saw a delightful portrait
of him.   It is from a copy of this picture that
the engraving in the " Gallery of Portraits," published by the Society for the Diffusion of Useful
Knowledge, is taken.   The face and air are worthy

of the man,—gentle and venerable. The philosopher's house we found occupied by a Judge and
his lady who are Quakers, while their children are
orthodox: but this double difference of religious
opinion does not impair their respect for the former
inhabitant of their dwelling. They preserve, with
an honourable reverence, every vestige of him and his
pursuits. They show the willows that were planted
in his time in the garden, and have preserved the
round hole he made in the window shutter of his
study, for the advantage of his optical experiments;
and even the bit of wainscot which he scorched with
his burning glasses. They took me to the corner of
the library where he breathed his last, and to the
balustrade on the top of the roof, where he went up
to meditate at eventide. It commands a beautiful
prospect of the course of the two branches of the
Susquehanna, and of their junction.

Priestley's Hill is so called from its vicinity to
the lands held by his family. It is pleasant to know
that he was possessed of abundance during the last
years of his life. His own wants were few; almost
all his expenditure being in charity and in his philosophical pursuits. He had enough for these, and
to settle his sons on good farms. No man bestowed
and accepted money with a better grace than he:
his generous English friends, who had the best reasons for being aware of this, had the satisfaction of

knowing that no pecuniary anxieties mingled with the trials of his closing years.

The tombs of the three,—of Priestley, his excellent wife, and his son Harry,—are in a family graveyard, which is on the outskirts of the little town, and some way from the family residence. It is walled round, and has an iron gate. I was familiar with the account of Harry's funeral, written at the time, and could not understand how it happened that he lay in this place. It is clear, from the testimony of persons on the spot, that his body had never been moved; and as the place of interment is described as being woodland, we must suppose that the bare place where he lies was within the verge of the forest in 1795. A resident in the neighbourhood wrote thus :—" I attended the funeral to the lonely spot, and there I saw the good old father perform the service over the grave of his son. It was an affecting sight, but he went through it with fortitude, and, after praying, addressed the attendants in a few words, assuring them that, though death had separated them here, they should meet again in another and a better world."

How little did I think when, some years ago, I read and re-read the narrative of Harry's death,— striving to extract from it something more, and yet something more to throw light on the character of father and son,—that I should stand by that very

grave, and plant a rose upon it! Few feet have
wandered that way; and no hands seem to have
been busied about those graves; but I was thankful
to be there, among the first of many pilgrims who
will yet see the spot. For another pupil of the
philosopher's, whose homage I carried with my own,
I planted a snow-berry on Priestley's grave. When
that other and I were infants, caring for nothing but
our baby plays, this grave was being dug for one
who was to exert a most unusual influence over our
minds and hearts, exercising our intellects, and winning our affections like a present master and parent,
rather than a thinker who had passed away from the
earth. Here I now stood by his grave, listening to
tales which seemed as fresh as if he were living and
walking yesterday, instead of having been wept before I knew any of the meanings of tears.

The inscription on Priestley's tomb is singularly
inappropriate—" Return unto thy rest, O my soul,
for the Lord hath dealt bountifully with thee. I
will lay me down in peace and sleep, until I awake
in the morning of the resurrection." Phrases from
the Old Testament, and about the soul, on the
grave of Priestley!

I remained in the neighbourhood several days,
and visited as many of the philosopher's haunts as
I could get pointed out to me; and when I was at
length obliged to resume my journey down the Sus-

quehannâ, it was with a strong feeling of satisfaction in the accomplishment of my object. These are the places in which to learn what are the real, in distinction from the comparatively insignificant, objects of regard;—of approbation and hatred;—of desire and fear. This was the place to learn what survived of a well-exercised and much-tried man. He made mistakes: they are transient evils, for others have been sent to rectify them. He felt certain of some things still dubious: this is a transient evil; for he is gone where he will obtain greater clearness; and men have arisen, and will arise, to enlighten us, and those who will follow us. He exploded errors: this was a real, but second-rate good, which would have been achieved by another if not by him. He discovered new truths: this is a real good, and as eternal as truth itself. He made an unusual progress towards moral perfection: this is the highest good of all, and never ending. His mistakes will be rectified; the prejudices against him on their account will die out: the hands that injured him, the tongues that wounded him, are all or nearly all stilled in death: the bitter tears which these occasioned have long since been all wept. These things are gone or going by; they have reached, or are tending to the extinction which awaits all sins and sorrows. What remains? Whatever was real of the man and of the work given him to do. Whatsoever truth he discovered will propagate itself for ever, whether the honour of it be ascribed to him or not. There remain other things no less great, no less real, no less eternal, to be reckoned among the spiritual treasures of the race; things of which Priestley, the immortal, was composed, and in which he manifestly survives: a love of truth which no danger could daunt, and no toil relax: a religious faith which no severity of probation could shake: a liberality proof against prejudice from within and injury from without: a simplicity which no experience of life and men could corrupt: a charity which grew tenderer under persecution, and warmer in exile: a hope which flourished in disappointment, and triumphed in the grave. These are the things which remain, bearing no relation to country or time; as truly here as there; now as hereafter.

These realities are the inheritance of those who sit at home, as well as of those who wander abroad: yet it may be forgiven to the weak, whose faith is dim-sighted, and whose affections crave a visible resting-place, if they find their sense of privilege refreshed by treading the shores of the exile's chosen Susquehanna.

PRISONS.

" In the prison of Coldbath Fields, in which the silent system is believed to be brought to the greatest degree of perfection, under the management of a highly intelligent and able governor, who has at his command every possible advantage for working the system, there were in the year 1836 no less than 5138 punishments ' for talking and swearing.' "—*Second Report of the Inspectors of Prisons of Great Britain*, 1837.

" Silence and Secrecy ! . . . Do thou thyself but hold thy tongue for one day ; on the morrow how much clearer are thy purposes and duties ! what wreck and rubbish have those mute workmen within thee swept away, when intrusive noises were shut out !"—*Sartor Resartus*.

I HAVE shown in my account of Society in America that, after visiting several prisons in the United States, I was convinced that the system of solitary confinement pursued at Philadelphia is the best that has yet been adopted.* So much has been heard in England of the Auburn prison, its details look so complete and satisfactory on paper, and it is so much a better system than the English have been accustomed to see followed at home, that it has a high reputation among us. But I think a careful survey of the institution on the spot must

* " Society in America," part. iii., chap. iv.

lessen the admiration entertained for this mode of punishment.

The convicts are, almost without exception, pale and haggard. As their work is done either in the open air, or in well-ventilated shops, and their diet is good, their unhealthy appearance is no doubt owing chiefly to the bad construction of their night-cells. These cells are small and ill-ventilated, and do not even answer the purpose of placing the prisoners in solitude during the night. The convicts converse with nearly as much ease, through the air-pipes or otherwise, at night, as they do by speaking behind their teeth, without moving the lips, while at work in the day. In both cases, they feel that they are transgressing the laws of the prison by doing an otherwise innocent, and almost necessary act : a knowledge and feeling most unfavourable to reformation, and destructive of any conscientiousness which retribution may be generating in them. Their anxious and haggard looks may be easily accounted for. They are denied the forgetfulness of themselves and their miseries which they might enjoy in free conversation ; and also the repose and the shelter from shame which are the privileges of solitary confinement. Every movement reminds them that they are in disgrace : a multitude of eyes (the eyes of the wicked, too,) is ever upon them : they can neither live to themselves nor to society, and self-respect is rendered next to impossible. A man must be either hardened, or restless and wretched, under such circumstances; and the faces at Auburn are no mystery.

The finishing of the day's work, and the housing for the night, are sights barely endurable. The governor saw my disgust, and explained that he utterly disapproved of strangers being allowed to be present at all this; but that the free Americans would not be debarred from witnessing the operation of any thing which they have decreed. This is right enough: the evil is in there being any such spectacle to witness.—The prisoners are ranged in companies for the march from their workshops into the prison. Each fills his pail and carries it, and takes up the can with his supper as he passes the kitchen; and, when I was there, this was done in the presence of staring and amused strangers, who looked down smiling from the portico. Some of the prisoners turned their heads every possible way to avoid meeting our eyes, and were in an agony of shame; while the blacks, who, from their social degradation, have little idea of shame, and who are remarkable for exaggeration in all they do, figured away ridiculously in the march, stamping and gesticulating as if they were engaged in a game at romps. I do not know which extreme was the most painful to witness. It is clear that no occasion should be afforded for either; that men should not be ignominiously paraded because they are guilty.

The arrangements for the women were extremely bad at that time; but the governor needed no convincing of this, and hoped for a speedy rectification. The women were all in one large room, sewing. The attempt to enforce silence was soon given up as hopeless; and the gabble of tongues among the few who were there was enough to paralyze any matron. Some rather hopeful-looking girls were side by side with old offenders of their own colour, and with some most brutish looking black women. There was an engine in sight which made me doubt the evidence of my own eyes,—stocks of a terrible construction; a chair, with a fastening for the head and for all the limbs. Any lunatic asylum ought to be ashamed of such an instrument. The governor liked it no better than we; but he pleaded that it was his only means of keeping his refractory female prisoners quiet, while he was allowed only one room to put them all into. I hope these stocks have been used for fire-wood before this.

The first principle in the management of the guilty seems to me to be to treat them as men and women; which they were before they were guilty, and will be when they are no longer so; and which they are in the midst of it all. Their humanity is the principal thing about them; their guilt is a temporary state. The insane are first men, and secondarily diseased men; and in a due consideration of this order of things lies the main secret of the successful treatment of such. The drunkard is first a man, and secondarily a man with a peculiar weakness. The convict is, in like manner, first a man, and then a sinner. Now, there is something in the isolation of the convict which tends to keep this order of considerations right in the mind of his guardians. The warden and his prisoner converse like two men when they are face to face : but when the keeper watches a hundred men herded together in virtue of the one common characteristic of their being criminals, the guilt becomes the prominent circumstance, and there is an end of the brotherly faith in each, to which each must mainly owe his cure. This, in our human weakness, is the great evil attendant upon the good of collecting together sufferers under any particular physical or moral evil. Visitors are shy of the blind, the deaf and dumb, and insane, when they see them all together, while they would feel little or nothing of this shyness if they met each sufferer in the bosom of his own family. In the one case, the infirmity, defying sympathy, is the prominent circumstance; in the other, not. It follows from this, that such an association of prisoners as that at Auburn must be more difficult to reform, more difficult to do the

State's duty by, than any number or kind of criminals who are classed by some other characteristic,
or not classed at all.

The wonderfully successful friend of criminals,
Captain Pillsbury, of the Weathersfield prison,
has worked on this principle, and owes his success
to it.   His moral power over the guilty is so
remarkable, that prison-breakers who can be confined nowhere else are sent to him, to be charmed
into staying their term out.   I was told of his treatment of two such.   One was a gigantic personage,
the terror of the country, who had plunged deeper
and deeper in crime for seventeen years.   Captain
Pillsbury told him when he came, that he hoped
he would not repeat the attempts to escape which
he had made elsewhere.   "It will be best," said
he, "that you and I should treat each other as well
as we can.   I will make you as comfortable as I
possibly can, and shall be anxious to be your friend;
and I hope you will not get me into any difficulty
on your account.   There is a cell intended for
solitary confinement: but we never use it; and I
should be very sorry ever to have to turn the key
upon anybody in it.   You may range the place as
freely as I do, if you will trust me as I shall trust
you."   The man was sulky, and for weeks showed
only very gradual symptoms of softening under the
operation of Captain Pillsbury's cheerful confidence.

At length, information was given to the Captain of this man's intention to break prison. The Captain called him, and taxed him with it : the man preserved a gloomy silence. He was told that it was now necessary for him to be locked up in the solitary cell, and desired to follow the Captain, who went first, carrying a lamp in one hand, and the key in the other. In the narrowest part of the passage, the Captain (who is a small, slight man,) turned round and looked in the face of the stout criminal. " Now," said he, " I ask you whether you have treated me as I deserve? I have done every thing I could think of to make you comfortable ; I have trusted you, and you have never given me the least confidence in return, and have even planned to get me into difficulty. Is this kind?— And yet I cannot bear to lock you up. If I had the least sign that you cared for me . . . ." The man burst into tears. " Sir," said he, " I have been a very devil these seventeen years : but you treat me like a man."—" Come, let us go back," said the Captain. The convict had the free range of the prison as before. From this hour, he began to open his heart to the Captain, and cheerfully fulfilled his whole term of imprisonment, confiding to his friend, as they arose, all impulses to violate his trust, and all facilities for doing so which he imagined he saw.

The other case was of a criminal of the same character, who went so far as to make the actual attempt to escape. He fell, and hurt his ancle very much. The Captain had him brought in, and laid on his bed, and the ancle attended to; every one being forbidden to speak a word of reproach to the sufferer. The man was sullen, and would not say whether the bandaging of his ancle gave him pain or not. This was in the night; and every one returned to bed when all was done. But the Captain could not sleep. He was distressed at the attempt, and thought he could not have fully done his duty by any man who would make it. He was afraid the man was in great pain. He rose, threw on his gown, and went with a lamp to the cell. The prisoner's face was turned to the wall, and his eyes were closed; but the traces of suffering were not to be mistaken. The Captain loosened and replaced the bandage, and went for his own pillow to rest the limb upon; the man neither speaking nor moving all the time. Just when he was shutting the door, the prisoner started up, and called him back. " Stop, Sir. Was it all to see after my ancle that you have got up ?"

" Yes, it was. I could not sleep for thinking of you."

" And you have never said a word of the way I have used you !"

" I do feel hurt with you, but I don't want to call you unkind while you are suffering as I am sure you are now."

The man was in an agony of shame and grief. All he asked was to be trusted again, when he should have recovered. He was freely trusted, and gave his generous friend no more anxiety on his behalf.

Captain Pillsbury is the gentleman who, on being told that a desperate prisoner had sworn to murder him speedily, sent for him to shave him, allowing no one to be present. He eyed the man, pointed to the razor, and desired him to shave him. The prisoner's hand trembled; but he went through it very well. When he had done, the Captain said, " I have been told you meant to murder me : but I thought I might trust you." " God bless you, Sir ! you may," replied the regenerated man. Such is the power of faith in man !

The greatest advantage of solitary confinement is, that it presents the best part of the prisoner's mind to be acted upon by his guardians ; and the next is, that the prisoner is preserved from the evil influences of vicious companionship, of shame within the prison walls, and of degradation when he comes out. I am persuaded that no system of secondary punishment has yet been devised that can be compared with this. I need not, at this time of day, explain that I mean solitary imprisonment with labour, and with frequent visits from the guardians of the prisoner. Without labour, the punishment is too horrible and unjust to be thought of. The reflective man would go mad, and the clown would sleep away his term ; and none of the purposes of human existence could be answered. Work is, in prison as out of it, the grand equaliser, stimulus, composer and rectifier; the prime obligation, and the prime privilege. It is delightful to see how soon its character is recognised there. In the Philadelphia penitentiary, work is forbidden to the criminal for two days subsequent to his entrance : he petitions for it before the two days are out, however doggedly he may have declared that he will never work. Small incidents show what a resource it is. A convict shoemaker mentioned to a visitor a very early hour of the winter day as that at which he began to work. " But how can you see at that time of a winter's morning ? it must be nearly dark."—" I hammer my leather. That requires very little light. I get up and hammer my leather."

On his entrance, the convict is taken to the bath-room, where he is well cleansed, and his state of health examined into and recorded by the physician and warden. A hood is then put over his head, and he is led to his apartment. I never met with

one who could in the least tell what the form of
the central part of the prison was, or which of the
radii his cell was placed in, though they make very
accurate observations of the times at which the sun
shines in. At the end of two days, during which
the convict has neither book nor work, the warden
visits him, and has a conversation with him about
the mode of life in the institution. If he asks for
work, he is offered a choice of three or four kinds,
of which weaving and shoe-making are the chief.
He is told that if he does a certain amount of work,
he will have the full diet provided for hard labourers;
if less, he will have what is sufficient for a moderate
worker; if more, the price of it will be laid by to
accumulate, and paid over to him on his leaving
the prison. He is furnished with a bible; and
other books, provided by friends to the institution,
circulate among the convicts. Some who have
books at home are allowed to have them brought.
A convict gentleman whom I visited had a fine
library at home, and was plentifully supplied from
thence. It was difficult to find occupation for this
unhappy man, who had never been used to labour.
He was filling bobbins when I saw him; and he
wrote a great deal in various languages. His story
was a dreadful one; too horrible to be related.
His crime was murder, but committed under such
intense provocation, real or imaginary, that he had

the compassion of every one who knew his history. He had been justice of the peace for twenty years ; and his interest was so strong that he had little doubt of being able to obtain a pardon, and for some years was daily racked with expectation. He told me that it was opposed by political enemies only ; and this belief did not, of course, tend to calm his mind. Pardon came at last, when nine years of the twelve for which he was sentenced had expired. He was released a year and a half after I saw him.

In his case there were peculiar disturbing influences, and his seclusion was doubtless more painful and less profitable than that of most prisoners. His case was public ; his station and the singularity of the circumstances made it necessarily so : and the knowledge of this publicity is a great drawback upon reformation, and upon repose of mind. The most hopeful cases I met with were those of men who came from a distance, who were tried under a feigned name, or whose old connexions were, from other circumstances, unaware of their present condition. Of course I cannot publicly relate facts concerning any of these. They disclosed their stories to me in confidence. I can give nothing but general impressions, except in a few cases which are already notorious, or where death has removed the obligation to secrecy, by rendering it impossible for the penitent to be injured, while his reputation may be benefited by its being known what were the feelings of his latter days.

After a general survey of the establishment, which furnished me with all that the managers had to bring forward, I entered, by the kind permission of the Board, upon the yet more interesting inquiry of what the convicts had to say for themselves. I supposed that, from their long seclusion from all society but that of their guardians, they would be ready to communicate very freely; and also, judging from my own feelings, that they could not do this in the presence of any third person. I therefore requested, and was allowed, to go entirely alone, the turnkey coming at the end of a specified time to let me out. No one of them, except the gentleman above mentioned, had any notice whatever of my coming. Their door was unlocked at an unusual hour, and I stepped in. My reception was, in every case, the same. Every man of them looked up, transfixed with amazement, one with his shuttle, another with his awl suspended. I said that if my visit was not agreeable, I would call the turnkey before he was out of hearing, and go away. If the contrary, perhaps I might be favoured with a seat. In an instant the workman sprang up, wiped his stool with his apron for me, and sat down himself on his work bench. In a few cases I had to make a further explanation that I did not come for prayer

and religious discourse. The conversation invariably took that turn before I left, as it naturally
does with the anxious and suffering; but two or
three rushed at once into such shocking cant, that I
lost no time in telling them the real object of my
visit,—to learn what were the causes of crime in
the United States. I also told them all that I could
not give them news from the city, because this was
against the rules of the prison. They were glad to
converse with me on my own conditions, and I am
confident that they presented me faithfully with
their state of mind, as it appeared to themselves.
I have never received confidence more full and
simple than theirs; and much of it was very extraordinary. All, except two or three, voluntarily
acknowledged their guilt—the last point, of course,
on which I should have chosen to press them. It
seemed a relief to them to dwell on the minutest
particulars relating to their temptation to their
crime, and the time and mode of its commission.
One man began protesting his innocence early in
our conversation; following the practice common
among felons, of declaring himself a guilty fellow
enough, but innocent of this particular crime. I
stopped him, saying that I asked him no questions,
and had no business with his innocence or guilt;
and that I did not like such protestations as he was
making : we would talk of something else. He

looked abashed; and within half an hour he had communicated his first act of dishonesty in life,— the festering wound which I have reason to believe he never before laid open to human eye.

Several incidents of this nature which occurred persuade me that almost anything may be done with these sufferers by occasional intercourse and free sympathy. Each time that I went I was amazed at the effect of words that had passed, lightly enough, days or weeks before. I found them all expecting a pardon ; and the most painful part of my duty to them was undeceiving them about this. It was dreadful to see the emotion of some : but I knew they would have no repose of mind, so necessary in their case, while racked with this hope : I therefore took pains to explain what punishment was for, and how rarely pardon could be justified. On my subsequent visits it was cheering to see how completely they had understood me, and how they had followed out the subject to their own entire conviction.

" Well, J.," said I to a young man who had been rather languid about his work, making only three shoes a week while expecting a pardon, " how have you been since I saw you?"

" Very fairly indeed, madam. I make seven shoes a week now."

" Ah! then you have left off fretting yourself

about a pardon. You have made up your mind to your term, like a man."

" Yes, I have been thinking about that,—and something more. I have been thinking that perhaps it is well that I am here now ; for, madam, I got that that I took so easily that I believe, if I had not been caught, I should have gone back to the same place, and taken more ; and so have come in for ten years instead of five."

Twenty months afterwards I heard of this man from the warden. He was in health, cheerful, and industrious. I have no doubt of his doing well when he comes out.

A negro, in for a very serious offence, which he acknowledged, told me of another committed long before, which, since his imprisonment, had weighed much more heavily on his mind, perhaps because no one knew it, or suspected him ; it was a theft of sixteen dollars, committed with some treachery. This subject had been entirely dismissed, and had even gone out of my mind when we talked over the expiration of his term, and his prospects in life. " Where do you mean to go first ?" said I. " Stay in Philadelphia till I have worked for those sixteen dollars, and paid them," said he. This was without the slightest leading on my part.

Several told me more about their mothers than about anything else in their former lives : and those

who were tried under false names seemed more
afraid of their mothers knowing where they were,
than of any other consequence. In every case
some heart-sore was at the bottom of the guilt.
Many were as ignorant as Americans ever are, and
had sought to get rid of their griefs, as ignorant
people do, by physical excitement. First, passion,
then drink, then crime : this is the descent. Most
declared that the privation of tobacco was the first
tremendous suffering within the prison; then the
solitude ; then the vain hope of pardon. The middle
part of their term is the easiest. Near the end they
grow restless and nervous. Every one that I asked
could promptly tell me the day of the month.

" May I ask," said I to one for whom I had
much regard, " may I ask what all these black
marks on your wall are for ? " I was not without a
conjecture, remembering that he was to go out on
the 17th of the next August; this being the 1st of
December.

He looked down, and said he had no secret in
the matter ; only that I should think him very silly.
I told him that I did not think any amusement
silly to one who had so few.

" Well, madam, I have been trying to find out
what day of the week the 17th of next August will
be: but I can't quite make it out, because I don't
know whether the next is leap year."

The holding out my hand to them at parting brought every one of them to tears : yet there was nothing unmanly in their bearing : there was no lack of health, no feebleness of spirits, though a quietness of manner such as might be anticipated in men under punishment, and subject to remorse. There was a degree of contentment (when the expectation of pardon was removed) which I did not look for. They spoke (such as were qualified) of other prisons with horror, and with approbation approaching to thankfulness of the treatment they met with in this, where they were not degraded as if they had done nothing but crime,—as if they were not still men. I was much moved by the temper of one ; and much humbled (as I often was) at thinking for how little guilt some are heavily visited, when there is not one of us, perhaps, who may not justly feel that, however safe and honoured he may appear, he has done worse, and deserved a more fearful retribution.

A friend of mine, who knew that I was visiting the penitentiary, asked me to see two brothers who were in for forging and coining. The case was notorious, the elder brother being an old offender. I agreed to inquire for them ; and upon this my friend somewhat imprudently told the mother of the convicts, and the wife of the younger one, what I had promised, and sent them to see me. I soon perceived that the wife was telling me a number of family particulars in the hope that I should communicate them to her husband. I felt myself obliged to put a stop to this, as I was upon honour, and could not think of violating any of the rules of the prison, one of which was that the convicts should receive no intelligence from without. The wife's reply was heart-wringing. She said she did not wish to show disrespect to any rules; there was but one thing that she implored me to convey to her husband. He had expected a pardon in three months from his conviction: five months had now passed, and he would be wondering. She only wanted him to know that it was through no want of exertion on her part that he was still in prison. I was compelled to refuse to communicate anything, and even to let the young man know that I had seen any of his family. But in my own mind I resolved not to see the convict till the warden, who was absent, should return to Philadelphia, and to tell him the whole, that he might communicate what he thought proper. By these means I believe the prisoner heard some comfortable tidings after I saw him, and I am sure he had never a hard thought of his good wife. I promised her a most minute account of her husband's situation, to which there could be no objection. She had done nothing wrong, and was not to be punished: though it appeared that some of the ladies of Philadelphia thought otherwise, as they took from her the needle-work she had undertaken for the support of herself and her children during her husband's imprisonment. These virtuous ladies could not think of countenancing any body connected with forgers and coiners.

I found the young man weaving. After some talk about the work, during which I saw that his mind was full of something else, I obviated all danger of his putting questions which I could not answer, by asking him whether he had relations in the city. This put an end to all reserve. He mentioned his father, and the brother who had led him into crime, with a forbearance and delicacy of forgiveness which were extremely touching. He was not aware that I knew how different a tone might have been excused,—might have been almost justified. But he spoke most of his wife. He told me that he had always been weak, too easily per-suaded, from being afraid of some people about him; and that his wife, who had a nobler mind, always kept him up; yet managing to do it when they were alone, so as never to expose his weakness. He had unfortunately come to Philadelphia two days before her; and in that interval he had been threatened and persuaded into endeavouring to pass two counterfeit five-franc pieces. This was .all.

But he himself did not extenuate his offence, or appear to think it a trifle. He observed indeed that at that time he was not aware what sins against property were: he used to think that if some people had so much more than they wanted, there was no great harm in those who have too little taking some from them. He had had much time for thought since, and now saw so plainly how necessary it was that men should be protected while living in society, that he believed no compulsion could now make him break the laws in any such way. But the mischief was done. He had made his wife wretched, and all was over. I convinced him that it was not. His term was five years; and when it was fulfilled, he would still be a young man, and might cherish his wife for many good years. It was well that we thought so at the time, for the hope gave him substantial comfort. He lifted up his head from his loom, where it had sunk down in his bitter weeping, and began to talk upon the subject I dreaded,— pardon. I saw what kind of mind I had to deal with,—reasoning and reflective. I led him to consider, as he had found out the purposes of law, the purposes of punishment; and at length put the question to him whether he thought he ought to be pardoned. Trembling from head to foot, and white as the wall, he bravely answered " No." I asked him whether it would not be better to settle his mind to his lot than to be trembling, for four years, at every footstep that came near his cell, expecting deliverance, and expecting it in vain. He did not answer. I told him that when he was heart-sick with expecting in vain, perhaps even some hard thought of his wife,—that she had not done all she could,—might rise up to trouble him. " O no, no, never !" he cried. I had now obtained what I wanted for her.

I told him I should endeavour to see his wife. He desired me to tell her that he was in health, and had brought himself to own to me what he had done ; and that he should be pretty comfortable but for thinking how he had used her : but he would try to make up for it one day. He was quite cheerful when I left him.

The wife called on me the next day. She said she could not stay long, as she was about to set off, with her children, for a remote part of the country. It was a dreadful thing to her to leave her husband's neighbourhood ; but she had been deprived of the means of support by her work being taken from her, and no resource remained but going to her father's house. She was surprised, and seemed almost sorry (no doubt from a jealousy for his reputation) that her husband had acknowledged his offence. She said he had not acknowledged it when he went in. I told her every particular about his

cell and employments, as well as his looks and conversation, till, when I had done, she started up,
saying that she was forgetting her children, and her
journey, and everything. When we had parted, she
came back again from the door, to ask " one thing
more ;"—whether I thought there would ever be
anything in the world that she could do for me. I
thought it very possible, in a world of change like
this; and promised to rely upon her, if she could
ever serve me or mine.

She settled herself at her father's, and after a
while drooped in spirits, and was sure something
would happen. When bad news came, she cried,
" There! I knew it." As the turnkey passed
her husband's cell, one day, he heard some noise,
and looked in. The young man was just falling from his loom in a fit of apoplexy. There
was no delay in doing all that can be done in such
cases; but in a few hours he died. There is no
reason to suppose that his imprisonment had anything to do with the attack. It was probably a
constitutional tendency, aggravated by anxiety of
mind.

The prison must be tried some years longer before a complete comparison of it with others can be
made: but it appears at present, that if there be
some few diseases which may possibly be aggravated
by the silence and thoughtfulness attendant on soli-

tary confinement (which I do not know to be the case,) there are many more which disappear under the regularity of temperature and of hours, and the good diet of the establishment. There was certainly less sallowness and anxiety in the faces of the inmates than struck me in the other prisons. One man amazed me by calling the four years he had passed here the most comfortable he had ever known; but when he told me the wretchedness of his previous life, I fully believed him.

I found, on visiting the elder of the brothers, how complete is the secrecy preserved in the prison. I had been repeatedly told that these brothers came in together, and therefore had no hesitation in mentioning the one to the other. I was thunderstruck with the vehemence with which the elder turned upon me with the question, " Is *my* brother in this prison?" " I was told you came in together," replied I. " Then they put him in just after me," cried he. " What did they find him guilty of? What part of the prison is he in? What work does he do?" and a number of other questions; none of which, of course, I would answer. I was not very sorry that he was accidentally made acquainted with what he had led his young brother into. I fear he could bear it only too well. When I told the warden the mistake I had made, I found that the younger brother came in three weeks after the elder.

The cases I became acquainted with were not all hopeful. Some of the convicts were so stupid as not to be relied upon, more or less. Others canted so detestably, and were (always in connexion with their cant) so certain that they should never sin more, that I have every expectation that they will find themselves in prison again some day. One fellow, a sailor, notorious for having taken more lives than probably any man in the United States, was quite confident that he should be perfectly virtuous hence-forth. He should never touch anything stronger than tea, or lift his hand against money or life. I told him I thought he could not be sure of all this till he was within sight of money and the smell of strong liquors; and that he was more confident than I should like to be. He shook his shock of red hair at me, and glared with his one ferocious eye, as he said he knew all about it, as he had been the worst of men, and Christ had had mercy on his poor soul. When I had got him away from his cant, and upon subjects on which he could talk with some simplicity, I found that even this man preferred this prison to others that he had been in. It so hap-pened that no conviction for murder had ever been procurable against him ; his imprisonments were all for theft. His account of the old Walnut-street prison was dreadful. He there daily heard stories of crimes, from four in the winter afternoons till daylight. " Poor boasting! for the crimes they bragged of were never done." I asked him how he got into that prison. " For a couple o' larcenies, a grand and a little," said he, with the most business-like nonchalance. He was waylaid by two old burglars on his coming out, and on the spot agreed upon an enterprise for the next night. His mother died in his arms : he went and committed the burglary, was caught, and before midnight was in prison again. His accounts of his deeds were too scientific for my understanding ; but I made out enough to be ready when he asked my advice what to do when he came out. I answered as if he were in earnest, advising him to leave Philadelphia and all towns, and settle in the woods, out of the way of grog-shops, bad company, and other people's property. But his keepers expect that he will end his days with them ; and this is the hope of that part of society which fears his ferocity.

As the system of solitary imprisonment gains ground, I trust that the practice of prison-visiting will gain ground too. It is most desirable that it should not be left wholly in the hands of proselyting religionists, but be shared by those who better understand human nature, and command a greater variety of influences. For the sake of religion itself this is desirable, to rescue it from becoming a mere prison solace ; an excitement seized when no other can be had, and to be laid aside when old pursuits offer themselves for resumption.   Kind-hearted persons will have an opportunity of doing extensive and unquestionable good by keeping up the social affections of the prisoners, giving them new ideas, making them cheerful, and investing with pleasant associations whatever things are honest, pure, lovely, and of good report.

In other prisons, much might thus be done, though not, I think, with such extraordinary effect as under the system of solitary confinement.   I was struck with something I saw at the Charlestown prison (Massachusetts).   Several convicts, black and white, who had behaved well, were practising singing, which is allowed as an indulgence.   It seemed strange to hear " The heavens are telling" from such lips : but I listened to it with more pleasure than in some far finer places.   Any kind person who can introduce a new innocent pursuit into a prison, as a solace to its inmates, cannot fail to be doing an important good.

This reminds me that a service may be rendered, not so much to the convicts as to society, by any persons who can supply the prisons where stone-cutting is going on with a good set of epitaphs.   At Auburn they are wanted, and much more at Nashville (Tennessee), where the stone-cutting department is superintended by an honest Englishman, whose stock of epitaphs is small, and of miserable quality. We half undertook to prepare and collect some for him, but found it a less easy task than we had supposed. We got out our pencils at three o'clock one summer morning, when our stage had broken down on a bad Tennessee road; but one of our party observing that this was the first time he had ever heard of making epitaphs for amusement, there was an end of the attempt; and the Nashville prison remains unsupplied, unless somebody else has done better than we.

I suspect the fault lies in the supposition that epitaphs of general application can be made at all. An epitaph should be the breathing of emotion arising out of a particular case; and none made for stone-cutters' use can have much life or truth. Still, they may have grammar and general propriety, so as to be an advantageous substitute for some at present in use, if only persons can be found to compose them on such considerations.

I saw at the Charlestown prison a sight more impressive to me than all else that the walls contained; a man of might, but whose power has taken a wrong direction; his hand being against every man, and every man's against him. He is a prison-breaker, so formidable as to be regarded and treated as if he were of Satanic race. and not as made up of flesh and blood, and emotions that may be roused, and affections subject to the touch. He seems indeed to have become somewhat of the Satanic kind, for he is now piqued to do all the harm he can. His pride is in for it : his reputation stands upon it. I was shown an enormous block of stone which he had displaced by the aid of a " gentleman" outside, who, for fear of the prison-breaker's blabbing, committed suicide on his recapture. The strong man was heavily fettered, confined in a different cell every night, and conducted to it by a procession of turnkeys. As we stood aside in the echoing passage to let the array go by, there was something really grand in the air of the man who had virtually said to himself " Evil, be thou my good !" He stepped slowly, clanking his chains, and looking us full in the face as he passed. He cannot but have a calm sense of power when he nightly sees the irons, the bars and locks, and the six fellow-men, all in requisition to keep him from working his will. As we saw him slowly turn into his cell, and heard lock after lock shot behind him, I could not help thinking that there was much true monarchical feeling within those four narrow walls.

FIRST SIGHT OF SLAVERY.

" Ed io, ch'avea di riguardar desio
  La condicion, che tal fortezza serra,
  Com' i fù dentro, l'occhio intorno invio,
  E veggio ad ogni man grande campagna
  Piena ad duolo, e di tormento rio."

Dante.

FROM the day of my entering the States till that of
my leaving Philadelphia, I had seen society basking
in one bright sunshine of good will. The sweet temper and kindly manners of the Americans are so
striking to foreigners, that it is some time before
the dazzled stranger perceives that, genuine as is all
this good, evils as black as night exist along with it.
I had been received with such hearty hospitality
everywhere, and had lived among friends so consci-
entious in their regard for human rights, that though
I had heard of abolition riots, and had observed
somewhat of the degradation of the blacks, my
mind had not yet been really troubled about the
enmity of the races. The time of awakening must
come. It began just before I left Philadelphia.

I was calling on a lady whom I had heard speak
with strong horror of the abolitionists (with whom I

had then no acquaintance) ; and she turned round upon me with the question whether I would not prevent, if I could, the marriage of a white person with a person of colour. I saw at once the beginning of endless troubles in this inquiry, and was very sorry it had been made : but my determination had been adopted long before, never to evade the great question of colour; never to provoke it ; but always to meet it plainly in whatever form it should be presented. I replied that I would never, under any circumstances, try to separate persons who really loved, believing such to be truly those whom God hath joined : but I observed that the case she put was one not likely to happen, as I believed the blacks were no more disposed to marry the whites than the whites to marry the blacks. " You are an amalgamationist ! " cried she. I told her that the party term was new to me; but that she must give what name she pleased to the principle I had declared in answer to her question. This lady is an eminent religionist, and denunciations spread rapidly from her. The day before I left Philadelphia, my old shipmate, the Prussian physician, arrived there, and lost no time in calling to tell me, with much agitation, that I must not go a step further south ; that he had heard on all hands, within two hours of his arrival, that I was an amalgamationist, and that my having published a story against

slavery would be fatal to me in the slave States.   I
did not give much credit to the latter part of this
news; and saw plainly that all I had to do was
to go straight on.   I really desired to see the working of the slave system, and was glad that my
having published against its principles divested me
altogether of the character of a spy, and gave me
an unquestioned liberty to publish the results
of what I might observe.   In order to see things as
they were, it was necessary that people's minds
should not be prepossessed by my friends as to my
opinions and conduct; and I therefore forbade my
Philadelphia friends to publish in the newspapers,
as they wished, an antidote to the charges already
current against me.

The next day I first set foot in a slave State,
arriving in the evening at Baltimore.   I dreaded
inexpressibly the first sight of a slave, and could
not help speculating on the lot of every person of
colour I saw from the windows, the first few days.
The servants in the house where I was were free
blacks.

Before a week was over, I perceived that all that
is said in England of the hatred of the whites to
the blacks in America is short of the truth.   The
slanders that I heard of the free blacks were too
gross to injure my estimation of any but those who
spoke them.   In Baltimore the bodies of coloured

people exclusively are taken for dissection, " because the whites do not like it, and the coloured people cannot resist." It is wonderful that the bodily structure can be (with the exception of the colouring of the skin) thus assumed to be the pattern of that of the whites ; that the exquisite nervous system, the instrument of moral as well as physical pleasures and pains, can be nicely investigated, on the ground of its being analogous with that of the whites ; that not only the mechanism, but the sensibilities of the degraded race should be argued from to those of the exalted order, and that men come from such a study with contempt for these brethren in their countenances, hatred in their hearts, and insult on their tongues. These students are the men who cannot say that the coloured people have not nerves that quiver under moral injury, nor a brain that is on fire with insult, nor pulses that throb under oppression. These are the men who should stay the hand of the rash and ignorant possessors of power who crush the being of creatures, like themselves, " fearfully and wonderfully made." But to speak the right word, to hold out the helping hand, these searchers into man have not light nor strength.

It was in Baltimore that I heard Miss Edgeworth denounced as a woman of no intelligence or delicacy, whose works could never be cared for again, because, in Belinda, poor Juba was married, at length, to an English farmer's daughter! The incident is so subordinate that I had entirely forgotten it: but a clergyman's lady threw the volume to the opposite corner of the floor when she came to the page. As I have said elsewhere, Miss Edgeworth is worshipped throughout the United States; but it is in spite of this terrible passage,—this clause of a sentence in Belinda,—which nobody in America can tolerate, while no one elsewhere ever, I should think, dreamed of finding fault with it.

A lady from New England, staying in Baltimore, was one day talking over slavery with me, her detestation of it being great, when I told her I dreaded seeing a slave. "You have seen one," said she. "You were waited on by a slave yesterday evening." She told me of a gentleman who let out and lent out his slaves to wait at gentlemen's houses, and that the tall handsome mulatto who handed the tea at a party the evening before was one of these. I was glad it was over for once; but I never lost the painful feeling caused to a stranger by intercourse with slaves. No familiarity with them, no mirth and contentment on their part ever soothed the miserable restlessness caused by the presence of a deeply-injured fellow-being. No wonder or ridicule on the spot avails anything to the stranger. He suffers, and must suffer from this, deeply and long, as surely as he is human and hates oppression.

The next slave that I saw, knowing that it was a slave, was at Washington, where a little negro child took hold of my gown in the passage of our boarding-house, and entered our drawing-room with me. She shut the door softly, as asking leave to stay. I took up a newspaper. She sat at my feet, and began amusing herself with my shoe-strings. Finding herself not discouraged, she presently begged play by peeping at me above and on each side the newspaper. She was a bright-eyed, merry-hearted child,—confiding, like other children, and dreading no evil, but doomed, hopelessly doomed to ignorance, privation, and moral degradation. When I looked at her, and thought of the fearful disobedience to the first of moral laws, the cowardly treachery, the cruel abuse of power involved in thus dooming to blight a being so helpless, so confiding, and so full of promise, a horror came over me which sickened my very soul. To see slaves is not to be reconciled to slavery.

At Baltimore and Washington again I was warned, in various stealthy ways, of perils awaiting me in the South. I had no means of ascertaining the justness of these warnings but by going on; and turning back for such vague reasons was not to be thought of. So I determined to say no word to my companions (who were in no danger), but to see the truth for myself. The threats proved idle, as I suspected they would. Throughout the South I met with very candid and kind treatment.—I mention these warnings partly because they are a fact connected with the state of the country; and partly because it will afterwards appear that the stranger's real danger lies in the north and west, over which the south had, in my case, greatly the advantage in liberality.

(235)

LIFE AT WASHINGTON.

" With studious thought observed the illustrious throng,
In Nature's order as they pass'd along;
Their names, their fates."
Dryden's Æneid.

WASHINGTON is no place for persons of domestic
tastes. Persons who love dissipation, persons who
love to watch the game of politics, and those who
make a study of strong minds under strong excite-
ments, like a season at Washington; but it is dreary
to those whose pursuits and affections are domestic.
I spent five weeks there, and was heartily glad
when they were over. I felt the satisfaction, all the
time, of doing something that was highly useful,—
of getting knowledge that was necessary to me,
and could not be otherwise obtained; but the quiet
delights of my Philadelphia home (though there
half our time was spent in visiting) had spoiled me
for such a life as every one leads at the metropolis.
I have always looked back upon the five weeks
at Washington as one of the most profitable, but
by far the least agreeable, of my residences in the
United States.

Yet we were remarkably fortunate in our domestic arrangements there. We joined a party of highly esteemed and kind friends,—a member of the House of Representatives from Massachusetts, his wife, and sister-in-law, and a Senator from Maine. We (the above party) had a drawing-room to ourselves, and a separate table, at Mrs. Peyton's boarding-house: so that we formed a quiet family group enough, if only we had had any quiet in which to enjoy the privilege.

We arrived at Washington on the 13th of January, 1835,—the year of the short session of Congress, which closes on the 4th of March; so that we continued to witness the proceedings of Congress at its busiest and most interesting time.

The approach to the city is striking to all strangers from its oddness. I saw the dome of the Capitol from a considerable distance, at the end of a straight road; but, though I was prepared by the descriptions of preceding travellers, I was taken by surprise on finding myself beneath the splendid building; so sordid are the enclosures and houses on its very verge. We wound round its base, and entered Pennsylvania Avenue, the only one of the grand avenues, intended to centre in the Capitol, which has been built up with any completeness. Our boarding-house was admirably situated, being some little way down this avenue, a few minutes'

walk only from the Capitol, and a mile in a straight
line from the White House, the residences of the
Heads of Departments, and the British Legation.

In Philadelphia, I had found perpetual difficulty
in remembering that I was in a foreign country.
The pronunciation of a few words by our host and
hostess, the dinner table, and the inquiries of
visiters were almost all that occurred to remind me
that I was not in a brother's house. At Washington, it was very different. The city itself is unlike
any other that ever was seen,—straggling out hither
and thither,—with a small house or two, a quarter
of a mile from any other; so that in making calls
"in the city," we had to cross ditches and stiles,
and walk alternately on grass and pavements, and
strike across a field to reach a street.—Then the
weather was so strange; sometimes so cold that the
only way I could get any comfort was by stretching
on the sofa drawn before the fire, up to the very
fender; (on which days, every person who went in
and out of the house was sure to leave the front
door wide open:) then the next morning, perhaps,
if we went out muffled in furs, we had to turn back,
and exchange our wraps for a light shawl. Then,
we were waited upon by a slave, appointed for the
exclusive service of our party during our stay. Then,
there were canvas-back ducks, and all manner of
other ducks on the table, in greater profusion than

any single article of food, except turkeys, that I
ever saw.   Then, there was the society, singularly
compounded from the largest variety of elements—
foreign ambassadors, the American government,
members of Congress, from Clay and Webster
down to Davy Crockett, Benton from Missouri,
and Cuthbert, with the freshest Irish brogue, from
Georgia ; flippant young belles, " pious" wives,
dutifully attending their husbands, and groaning
over the frivolities of the place; grave judges,
saucy travellers, pert newspaper reporters, melancholy Indian chiefs, and timid New England ladies,
trembling on the verge of the vortex,—all this was
wholly unlike any thing that is to be seen in any
other city in the world; for all these are mixed up
together in daily intercourse, like the higher circle
of a little village, and there is nothing else.   You
have this or nothing; you pass your days among
these people, or you spend them alone.   It is in
Washington that varieties of manners are conspicuous.   There the Southerners appear to the
most advantage, and the New Englanders to the
least: the ease and frank courtesy of the gentry of
the south, (with an occasional touch of arrogance,
however,) contrasting favourably with the cautious,
somewhat *gauche,* and too deferential air of the
members from the north.   One fancies one can tell
a New England member in the open air by his

deprecatory walk.   He seems to bear in mind
perpetually that he cannot fight a duel, while other
people can.   The odd mortals that wander in from
the western border cannot be described as a class;
for no one is like anybody else.   One has a neck
like a crane, making an interval of inches between
stock and chin.   Another wears no cravat, apparently because there is no room for one.   A third
has his lank black hair parted accurately down the
middle, and disposed in bands in front, so that he
is taken for a woman when only the head is seen in
a crowd.   A fourth puts an arm round the neck of
a neighbour on either side as he stands, seeming
afraid of his tall wire-hung frame dropping to
pieces if he tries to stand alone: a fifth makes
something between a bow and a curtsey to every
body who comes near, and proses with a knowing
air:—all having shrewd faces, and being probably
very fit for the business they come upon.

Our way of life was so diversified that it is difficult
to give an account of our day; the only way in which
one day resembled another being that none had any
privacy.   We breakfasted about nine, surrounded
by the heaps of newspapers, documents and letters
which the post and newsmen brought to the parliamentary members of our party.   We amused
ourselves with the different versions given by the
Globe and the Intelligencer,—the administration

and opposition papers,—to speeches and proceedings
at which we had been present the day before; and
were kindly made acquainted by our representative
friend with the nature of much of his business, the
petitions he had to present, the dilemmas in which
he was placed by his constituents of different parties,
and his hopes and fears about favorite measures in
progress. The senator happened, from a peculiar
set of circumstances, to be an idle man just now.
He taught me many things, and rallied me on my
asking him so few questions, while, in fact, my
head was already so much too full with what was
flowing in upon me from all sides, that I longed
for nothing so much as to go to sleep for a week.—
This gentleman's peculiar and not very agreeable
position arose out of the troublesome question
of Instructions to Representatives. Senators are
chosen for a term of six years, one-third of the
body going out every two years; the term being
made thus long in order to ensure some stability of
policy in the senate. If the government of the
State from which the senator is sent changes its
politics during his term, he may be annoyed by
instructions to vote contrary to his principles, and,
if he refuses, by a call to resign, on the ground of
his representing the opinions of the minority. This
had been the predicament of our companion; and
the question of resigning or not under such circum-

stances had become generally a very important and interesting one; but one which there were no means of settling. Each member, in such a scrape, must act as his own judgment and conscience dictate under the circumstances of the particular case. Our companion made a mistake. When the attempt to instruct him was made, he said he appealed from the new legislature of his State to the people who chose him. He did appeal by standing candidate for the office of Governor of the State, and was defeated. No course then remained but resigning; which he did immediately, when his senatorial term was within half a session of its close. He had withdrawn from the Senate Chamber, and was winding up his political affairs at the time when we joined his party.

At a little before eleven, we usually set out for the Capitol, and passed the morning either in the Senate Chamber or the Supreme Court, unless it was necessary to make calls, or to sit to the artist who was painting my portrait, or to join a party in some excursion in the neighbourhood. We avoided spending the morning at home, when we could, as it was sure to be entirely consumed with callers: and we became too much exhausted before the fatigues of the evening began. Much amusement was picked up in the artist's apartment in the Capitol: members and strangers dropped in, and

the news of the hour circulated : but the Senate
Chamber was our favourite resort. We returned
home to dinner some time between four and six, and
the cloth was seldom removed before visitors entered.
The stream continued to flow in during the whole
evening, unless we were all going out together. We
disappeared, one by one, to dress for some ball, rout,
levee, or masquerade, and went out, more or less
willingly, according as we left behind us visitors
more or less pleasant. The half-hour round our
drawing-room fire, after our return, was the pleasantest time of the day, weary as we were. Then
our foreigners' perplexities were explained for us ;
we compared impressions, and made common property of what had amused us individually ; and, in
some sort, set our overcharged minds in order, before
we retired to rest.

Our pleasantest evenings were some spent at
home in a society of the highest order. Ladies,
literary, fashionable, or domestic, would spend an
hour with us on their way from a dinner, or to a
ball. Members of Congress would repose themselves by our fire side. Mr. Clay, sitting upright
on the sofa, with his snuff-box ever in his hand,
would discourse for many an hour, in his even, soft,
deliberate tone, on any one of the great subjects of
American policy which we might happen to start,
always amazing us with the moderation of estimate

and speech which so impetuous a nature has been able to attain. Mr. Webster, leaning back at his ease, telling stories, cracking jokes, shaking the sofa with burst after burst of laughter, or smoothly discoursing to the perfect felicity of the logical part of one's constitution, would illuminate an evening now and then. Mr. Calhoun, the cast-iron man, who looks as if he had never been born, and never could be extinguished, would come in sometimes to keep our understandings upon a painful stretch for a short while, and leave us to take to pieces his close, rapid, theoretical, illustrated talk, and see what we could make of it. We found it usually more worth retaining as a curiosity than as either very just or useful. His speech abounds in figures, truly illustrative, if that which they illustrate were but true also. But his theories of government, (almost the only subject on which his thoughts are employed,) the squarest and compactest theories that ever were made, are composed out of limited elements, and are not therefore likely to stand service very well. It is at first extremely interesting to hear Mr. Calhoun talk; and there is a never failing evidence of power in all he says and does, which commands intellectual reverence: but the admiration is too soon turned into regret,—into absolute melancholy. It is impossible to resist the conviction that all this force can be at best but useless, and is but too likely to be very mischievous. His mind has long lost all power of communicating with any other. I know no man who lives in such utter intellectual solitude. He meets men and harangues them, by the fire-side, as in the Senate : he is wrought, like a piece of machinery, set a-going vehemently by a weight, and stops while you answer : he either passes by what you say, or twists it into a suitability with what is in his head, and begins to lecture again. Of course, a mind like this can have little influence in the Senate, except by virtue, perpetually wearing out, of what it did in its less eccentric days : but its influence at home is to be dreaded. There is no hope that an intellect so cast in narrow theories will accommodate itself to varying circumstances : and there is every danger that it will break up all that it can, in order to remould the materials in its own way. Mr. Calhoun is as full as ever of his Nullification doctrines ; and those who know the force that is in him, and his utter incapacity of modification by other minds, (after having gone through as remarkable a revolution of political opinion as perhaps any man ever experienced,) will no more expect repose and self-retention from him than from a volcano in full force. Relaxation is no longer in the power of his will. I never saw any one who so completely gave me the idea of possession. Half an hour's conversation with him is enough to make a necessarian of any body. Accordingly, he is more complained of than blamed by his enemies. His moments of softness, in his family, and when recurring to old college days, are hailed by all as a relief to the vehement working of the intellectual machine; a relief equally to himself and others. Those moments are as touching to the observer as tears on the face of a soldier.

One incident befel during my stay which moved every body.—A representative from South Carolina was ill, a friend of Mr. Calhoun's; and Mr. Calhoun parted from us, one day, on leaving the Capitol, to visit this sick gentleman. The physician told Mr. Calhoun on his entrance that his friend was dying, and could not live more than a very few hours. A visitor, not knowing this, asked the sick man how he was. " To judge by my own feelings," said he, " much better; but by the countenances of my friends, not." And he begged to be told the truth. On hearing it, he instantly beckoned Mr. Calhoun to him, and said, " I hear they are giving you rough treatment in the Senate. Let a dying friend implore you to guard your looks and words so as that no undue warmth may make you appear unworthy of your principles." " This was friendship,—strong friendship," said Mr. Calhoun to me, and to many others; and it had its due effect upon him. A few days after, Colonel Benton, a fantastic senator from Missouri, interrupted Mr. Calhoun in a speech, for the purpose of making an attack upon him, which would have been insufferable, if it had not been too absurdly worded to be easily made anything of. He was called to order; this was objected to; the Senate divided upon the point of order, being dissatisfied with the decision of the chair;—in short, Mr. Calhoun sat for two full hours, hearing his veracity talked about, before his speech could proceed. He sat in stern patience, scarcely moving a muscle the whole time; and when it was all settled in his favour, merely observed that his friends need not fear his being disturbed by an attack of this nature from such a quarter, and resumed his speech at the precise point where his argument had been broken off. It was great, and would have satisfied the " strong friendship " of his departed comrade, if he could have been there to witness it.

Our active-minded, genial friend, Judge Story, found time to visit us frequently, though he is one of the busiest men in the world,—writing half-a-dozen great law books every year, having his full share of the business of the Supreme Court upon his hands; his professorship to attend to; the District Courts at home in Massachusetts, and a correspondence which spreads half over the world. His talk would gush out for hours, and there was never too much of it for us ; it is so heartfelt, so lively, so various ; and his face all the while, notwithstanding his grey hair, showing all the mobility and ingenuousness of a child's. There is no tolerable portrait of Judge Story, and there never will be. I should like to bring him face to face with a person who entertains the common English idea of how an American looks and behaves. I should like to see what such an one would make of the quick smiles, the glistening eye, the gleeful tone, with passing touches of sentiment; the innocent self-complacency, the confiding, devoted affections of the great American lawyer. The preconception would be totally at fault.

With Judge Story sometimes came the man to whom he looked up with feelings little short of adoration; the aged Chief-Justice Marshall. There was almost too much mutual respect in our first meeting : we knew something of his individual merits and services; and he maintained through life, and carried to his grave, a reverence for woman as rare in its kind as in its degree. It had all the theoretical fervour and magnificence of Uncle Toby's, with the advantage of being grounded upon an extensive knowledge of the sex. He was the father and the grandfather of women; and out of this experience he brought, not only the love and pity which their offices and position command, and

the awe of purity which they excite in the minds of
the pure, but a steady conviction of their intellectual
equality with men; and, with this, a deep sense
of their social injuries.   Throughout life he so
invariably sustained their cause, that no indulgent
libertine dared to flatter and humour, no sceptic,
secure in the possession of power, dared to scoff at
the claims of woman in the presence of Marshall,
who, made clear-sighted by his purity, knew the sex
far better than either.

How delighted we were to see Judge Story bring
in the tall, majestic, bright-eyed old man !—old by
chronology, by the lines on his composed face, and
by his services to the republic; but so dignified, so
fresh, so present to the time, that no feeling of com-
passionate consideration for age dared to mix with
the contemplation of him.   The first evening, he
asked me much about English politics, and especially whether the people were not fast ripening for
the abolition of our religious establishment—an
institution which, after a long study of it, he considered so monstrous in principle, and so injurious
to true religion in practice, that he could not imagine
that it could be upheld for anything but political
purposes.   There was no prejudice here, on account
of American modes being different; for he observed
that the clergy were there, as elsewhere, far from
being in the van of society, and lamented the exist-

ence of much fanaticism in the United States: but he saw the evils of an establishment the more clearly, not the less, from being aware of the faults in the administration of religion at home. The most animated moment of our conversation was when I told him I was going to visit Mr. Madison, on leaving Washington. He instantly sat upright in his chair, and with beaming eyes began to praise Mr. Madison. Madison received the mention of Marshall's name in just the same manner: yet these men were strongly opposed in politics, and their magnanimous appreciation of each other underwent no slight or brief trial.

Judge Porter sometimes came, a hearty friend, and much like a fellow-countryman, though he was a senator of the United States, and had previously been, for fourteen years, Judge of the Supreme Court of Louisiana. He was Irish by birth. His father was vindictively executed, with cruel haste, under martial law, in the Irish rebellion; and the sons were sent by their noble-minded mother to America, where Alexander, the eldest, has thus raised himself into a station of high honour. Judge Porter's warmth, sincerity, generosity, knowledge, and wit are the pride of his constituents, and very ornamental to the Senate. What their charm is by the fireside may be imagined.

Such are only a few among a multitude whose

conversation filled up the few evenings we spent at
home.   Among the pleasantest visits we paid were
dinners at the President's, at the houses of Heads
of Departments, at the British Legation, and at the
southern members' congressional mess.   We highly
enjoyed our dinings at the British Legation, where
we felt ourselves at home among our countrymen.
Once indeed we were invited to help to do the honours
as English ladies, to the seven Judges of the Supreme
Court, and seven great lawyers besides, when we
had the merriest day that could well be.   Mr.
Webster fell chiefly to my share, and there is no
merrier man than he ; and Judge Story would
enliven a dinner table at Pekin.   One laughable
peculiarity at the British Legation was the confusion of tongues among the servants, who ask you to
take fish, flesh, and fowl in Spanish, Italian, German, Dutch, Irish, or French.   The foreign
ambassadors are terribly plagued about servants.
No American will wear livery; and there is no
reason why any American should.   But the British
ambassador must have livery servants.   He makes
what compromise he can, allowing his people to
appear without livery out of doors, except on state
occasions; but yet he is obliged to pick up his
domestics from among foreigners who are in want
of a subsistence for a short time, and are sure to go
away as soon as they can find any employment in

which the wearing a livery is not requisite. The woes of this state of things, however, were the portion of the host, not of his guests; and the hearty hospitality with which we were ever greeted by the minister and his attachés, combined with the attractions of the society they brought together, made our visits to them some of the pleasantest hours we passed in Washington.

Slight incidents were perpetually showing, in an amusing way, the village-like character of some of the arrangements at Washington. I remember that some of our party went one day to dine at Mr. Secretary Cass's, and the rest of us at Mr. Secretary Woodbury's. The next morning a lady of the Cass party asked me whether we had candied oranges at the Woodburys'. " No." " Then," said she, " they had candied oranges at .the Attorney-General's." " How do you know?" " O, as we were on the way, I saw a dish carried; and, as we had none at the Cass's, I knew they must be either for the Woodburys or the Attorney-General." There were candied oranges at the Attorney-General's.

When we became intimate, some time afterwards, with some southern friends with whom we now dined at their congressional mess, they gave us an amusing account of the preparations for our dinner. They boarded (from a really self-denying kindness) at a

house where the arrangements were of a very infe-
rior kind.   Two sessions previous to our being there
they had invited a large party of eminent persons
to dinner, and had committed the ordering of the
arrangements to a gentleman of their mess, advising
him to engage a French cook, in order to ensure a
good dinner.   The gentleman engaged a French-
man, concluding he must be a cook; which however
he was not; and the dinner turned out so unfortunately, that the mess determined to ask no more
dinner company while they remained in that house.
When we arrived, however, it was thought necessary
to ask us to dinner.   There was little hope that all
would go rightly; and the two senators of the mess
were laughingly requested, in case of any blunder,
to talk Nullification as fast as possible to us ladies.
This was done so efficaciously, that when dinner
was over, I could not have told a single dish that
was on the table, except that a ham stood before
me, which we were too full of Nullification to
attack.   Our hosts informed us, long afterwards,
that it was a bad dinner, badly served: but it was
no matter.

At the President's I met a very large party,
among whom there was more stiffness than I witnessed in any other society in America.   It was not
the fault of the President or his family, but of the
way in which the company was unavoidably brought

together. With the exception of my party, the
name of every body present began with J, K, or L:
that is to say, it consisted of members of Congress,
who are invited alphabetically, to ensure none being
left out. This principle of selection is not perhaps the best for the promotion of ease and soci-
ability ; and well as I liked the day, I doubt
whether many others could say they enjoyed it.
When we went in, the President was standing
in the middle of the room to receive his guests.
After speaking a few words with me, he gave me
into the charge of Major Donelson, his secretary,
who seated me, and brought up for introduction
each guest as he passed from before the President.
A congressional friend of mine (whose name began
with a J,) stationed himself behind my chair, and
gave me an account of each gentleman who was
introduced to me ;—where he came from, what his
politics were, and how, if at all, he had distinguished himself. All this was highly amusing.
At dinner, the President was quite disposed for
conversation. Indeed, he did nothing but talk.
His health is poor, and his diet of the sparest.
We both talked freely of the governments of England and France ; I, novice in American politics as
I was, entirely forgetting that the great French
question was pending, and that the President and
the King of the French were then bandying very

hard words. I was most struck and surprised with
the President's complaints of the American Senate,
in which there was at that time a small majority
against the administration. He told me that I
must not judge of the body by what I saw it then;
and that after the 4th of March I should behold a
Senate more worthy of the country. After the 4th
of March there was, if I remember rightly, a
majority of two in favour of the Government. The
ground of his complaint was, that the senators had
sacrificed their dignity by disregarding the wishes
of their constituents. The other side of the question is, that the dignity of the Senate is best con-
sulted by its members following their own convictions,
declining instructions for the term for which they
are elected. It is a serious difficulty, originating in
the very construction of the body, and not to be
settled by dispute.

The President offered me bonbons for a child belonging to our party at home, and told me how
many children (of his nephew's and his adopted
son's) he had about him, with a mildness and kindliness which contrasted well with his tone upon some
public occasions. He did the honours of his house
with gentleness and politeness to myself, and, as far
as I saw, to every one else. About an hour after
dinner, he rose, and we led the way into the drawing-room, where the whole company, gentlemen as

well as ladies, followed to take coffee; after which, every one departed; some homewards, some to make evening calls, and others, among whom were ourselves, to a splendid ball, at the other extremity of the city.

General Jackson is extremely tall and thin, with a slight stoop, betokening more weakness than naturally belongs to his years. He has a profusion of stiff grey hair, which gives to his appearance whatever there is of formidable in it. His countenance bears commonly an expression of melancholy gravity; though when roused, the fire of passion flashes from his eyes, and his whole person looks then formidable enough. His mode of speech is slow and quiet; and his phraseology sufficiently betokens that his time has not been passed among books. When I was at Washington, albums were the fashion and the plague of the day. I scarcely ever came home, but I found an album on my table, or requests for autographs; but some ladies went much further than petitioning a foreigner, who might be supposed to have leisure. I have actually seen them stand at the door of the Senate Chamber, and send the doorkeeper, with an album, and a request to write in it, to Mr. Webster, and other eminent members. I have seen them do worse; stand at the door of the Supreme Court, and send in their albums to Chief-Justice Marshall, while he was on the bench, hearing pleadings. The poor President was terribly persecuted; and to him it was a real nuisance, as he had no poetical resource but Watts's hymns. I have seen verses and stanzas of a most ominous purport from Watts, in the President's very conspicuous hand-writing, standing in the midst of the crow-quill compliments and translucent charades which are the staple of albums. Nothing was done to repress this atrocious,impertinence of the ladies. I always declined writing more than name and date; but senators, Judges and statesmen submitted to write gallant nonsense at the request of any woman who would stoop to desire it.

Colonel Johnson, now Vice-President of the United States, sat opposite to me at the President's dinner-table. This is the gentleman once believed to have killed Tecumseh, and to have written the Report on Sunday Mails, which has been the admiration of society ever since it appeared: but I believe Colonel Johnson is no longer supposed to be the author of either of these deeds. General Mason spoke of him to me at New York with much friendship, and with strong hope of his becoming President. I heard the idea so ridiculed by members of the federal party afterwards, that I concluded General Mason to be in the same case with hundreds more who believe their intimate friends sure of being President. But Colonel Johnson is actually Vice-

President, and the hope seems reasonable; though the slavery question will probably be the point on which the next election will turn, which may again be to the disadvantage of the Colonel. If he should become President, he will be as strange-looking a potentate as ever ruled. His countenance is wild, though with much cleverness in it; his hair wanders all abroad, and he wears no cravat. But there is no telling how he might look if dressed like other people.

I was fortunate enough once to catch a glimpse of the invisible Amos Kendall, one of the most remarkable men in America. He is supposed to be the moving spring of the whole administration; the thinker, planner and doer; but it is all in the dark. Documents are issued of an excellence which prevents their being attributed to persons who take the responsibility of them; a correspondence is kept up all over the country for which no one seems to be answerable; work is done, of goblin extent and with goblin speed, which makes men look about them with a superstitious wonder; and the invisible Amos Kendall has the credit of it all. President Jackson's Letters to his Cabinet are said to be Kendall's: the Report on Sunday Mails is attributed to Kendall: the letters sent from Washington to appear in remote country newspapers, whence they are collected and published in the Globe as demon-

strations of public opinion, are pronounced to be
written by Kendall. Every mysterious paragraph
in opposition newspapers relates to Kendall : and it
is some relief to the timid that his having now the
office of Postmaster-General affords opportunity for
open attacks upon this twilight personage; who
is proved, by the faults in the Post-Office administration, not to be able to do quite everything well.
But he is undoubtedly a great genius. He unites
with his " great talent for silence" a splendid audacity. One proof of this I have given elsewhere, in
the account of the bold stroke by which he obtained
the sanction of the Senate to his appointment as
Postmaster-General.*

It is clear that he could not do the work he does
(incredible enough in amount any way) if he went
into society like other men. He did, however, one
evening,—I think it was at the Attorney-General's.
The moment I went in, intimations reached me from
all quarters, amidst nods and winks, " Kendall is
here :" " That is he." I saw at once that his plea
for seclusion,—bad health,—is no false one. The
extreme sallowness of his complexion, and hair of
such perfect whiteness as is rarely seen in a man of
middle age, testified to disease. His countenance
does not help the superstitious to throw off their

* " Society in America," vol. i., p. 60.

dread of him. He probably does not desire this superstition to melt away; for there is no calculating how much influence was given to Jackson's administration by the universal belief that there was a concealed eye and hand behind the machinery of government, by which everything could be foreseen, and the hardest deeds done. A member of Congress told me, this night, that he had watched through four sessions for a sight of Kendall, and had never obtained it till now. Kendall was leaning on a chair, with head bent down, and eye glancing up at a member of Congress with whom he was in earnest conversation: and in a few minutes, he was gone.

Neither Mr. Clay nor any of his family ever spoke a word to me of Kendall, except in his public capacity: but I heard elsewhere and repeatedly the well-known story of the connexion of the two men, early in Kendall's life. Tidings reached Mr. and Mrs. Clay, one evening, many years ago, at their house in the neighbourhood of Lexington, Kentucky, that a young man, solitary and poor, lay ill of a fever in the noisy hotel in the town. Mrs. Clay went down in the carriage without delay, and brought the sufferer home to her house, where she nursed him with her own hands till he recovered. Mr. Clay was struck with the talents and knowledge of the young man (Kendall), and retained him as tutor to his sons, heaping benefits upon him with characteristic bounty. Thus far is notorious fact. As to the causes of their separation and enmity, I have not heard Kendall's side of the question; and I therefore say nothing; but go on to the other notorious facts, that Amos Kendall quitted Mr. Clay's political party some time after Adams had been, by Mr. Clay's influence, seated in the Presidential chair, and went over to Jackson; since which time, he has never ceased his persecutions of Mr. Clay through the newspapers. It was extensively believed, on Mr. Van Buren's accession, that Kendall would be dismissed from office altogether; and there was much speculation about how the administration would get on without him. But he appears to be still there. Whether he goes or stays, it will probably be soon apparent how much of the conduct of Jackson's government is attributable to Kendall's influence over the mind of the late President; as he is hardly likely to stand in the same relation to the present.

I was more vividly impressed with the past and present state of Ireland while I was in America than ever I was at home. Besides being frequently questioned as to what was likely to be done for the relief of her suffering millions,—suffering to a degree that it is inconceivable to Americans that free-born whites should ever be,—I met from time to

time with refugee Irish gentry, still burning with
the injuries they or their fathers sustained in the
time of the rebellion. The subject first came up
with Judge Porter: and I soon afterwards saw, at a
country-house where I was calling, the widow of
Theobald Wolfe Tone. The poor lady is still full
of feelings which amazed me by their bitterness and
strength; but which have indeed nothing surprising
in them to those who know the whole truth of the
story of Ireland in those dreadful days. The de-
scendants of " the rebels" cannot be comforted with
tidings of any thing to be done for their country.
Naturally believing that nothing good can come out
of England,—nothing good for Ireland,—they pas-
sionately ask that their country shall be left to govern
herself. With tears and scornful laughter, they beg
that nothing may be " done for her," by hands that
have ravaged her with gibbet, fire and sword, but
that she may be left to whatever hopefulness may
yet be smouldering under the ashes of her despair.
Such is the representation of Ireland to American
minds. It may be imagined what a monument of
idiotcy the forcible maintenance of the Church of
England in Ireland must appear to American statesmen. " I do not understand this Lord John Rus·
sell of yours," said one of the most sagacious of
them. " Is he serious in supposing that he can
allow a penny of the revenues, a plait of the lawn-

sleeves of that Irish Church to be touched, and keep the whole from coming down, in Ireland first, and in England afterwards?" We fully agreed in the difficulty of supposing Lord John Russell serious. The comparison of various, but I believe pretty extensive American opinions about the Church of England yields rather a curious result. No one dreams of the Establishment being necessary, or being designed for the maintenance of religion: it is seen by Chief-Justice Marshall and a host of others to be an institution turned to political purposes. Mr. Van Buren, among many, considers that the Church has supported the State for many years. Mr. Clay, and a multitude with him, anticipates the speedy fall of the Establishment. The result yielded by all this is a persuasion not very favourable (to use the American phrase) " to the permanence of our institutions."

Among our casual visitors at Washington was a gentleman who little thought, as he sat by our fireside, what an adventure was awaiting him among the Virginia woods. If there could have been any anticipation of it, I should have taken more notice of him than I did: as it is, I have a very slight recollection of him. He came from Maine, and intended before his return to visit the Springs of Virginia, which he did the next summer. It seems that he talked in the stages rashly, and somewhat in a

bragging style,—in a style at least which he was
not prepared to support by a harder testimony,—
about abolitionism.   He declared that abolitionism
was not so dangerous as people thought; that he
avowed it without any fear; that he had frequently
attended abolition meetings in the North, and was
none the worse for it in the Slave States, &c.   He
finished his visit at the Springs prosperously enough :
but on his return, when he and a companion were
in the stage, in the midst of the forest, they met at a
cross-road—Judge Lynch; that is, a mob with hints
of cowhide and tar and feathers.   The mob stopped
the stage, and asked for the gentleman by name.
It was useless to deny his name; but he denied
everything else.   He denied his being an abolitionist; he denied his having ever attended abolition
meetings, and harangued against abolitionism, from
the door of the stage, with so much effect that the
mob allowed the steps to be put up, and the vehicle
to drive off,—which it did at full speed.   It was
not long before the mob became again persuaded
that this gentleman was a fit object of vengeance,
and pursued him; but he was gone, as fast as horses
could carry him.   He did not relax his speed, even
when out of danger, but fled all the way into Maine.
It was not on the shrinking at the moment that one
would animadvert, so much as on the previous bragging.   I have seen and felt enough of what peril

from popular hatred is, in this martyr age of the United States, to find it easier to venerate those who can endure, than to despise those who flinch from the ultimate trial of their principles; but every instance of the infliction of Lynch punishment should be a lesson to the sincerest and securest, to profess no more than they are ready to perform.

One of our mornings was devoted to an examination of the library and curiosities of the State Department, which we found extremely interesting. Our imaginations were whirled over the globe at an extraordinary rate.   There were many volumes of original letters of Washington's, and other revolutionary leaders, bound up, and ordered to be printed, for security, lest these materials of history should be destroyed by fire, or other accident.   There were British parliamentary documents.   There was a series of the Moniteur complete; wherein we found the black list of executions, during the reign of terror, growing longer every day; also the first mention of Napoleon; the tidings of his escape from Elba; the misty days immediately succeeding, when no telegraphic communication could be made; his arrival at Lyons, and the subsequent silence till the announcement became necessary, that the king and princes had departed during the night, and that his Majesty, the Emperor, had arrived at his palace of the Tuilleries at eight o'clock the next evening.

Next we turned to Algerine (French) gazettes, publishing that mustaphas and such people were made colonels and adjutants.—Then we lighted upon the journals of Arnold, during the revolutionary war, and read the postscript of his last letter previous to the accomplishment of his treason, in which he asks for hard cash, on pretence that the French had suffered so much by paper-money, that he was unwilling to offer them any more.—Then we viewed the signatures of treaties, and decreed Metternich's to be the best; Don Pedro's the worst for flourish, and Napoleon's for illegibility. The extraordinary fact was then and there communicated to us that the Americans are fond of Miguel, from their dislike of Pedro; but that they hope to "get along" very well with the Queen of Portugal. The treaties with oriental potentates are very magnificent,—shining and unintelligible to the eyes of novices.—The presents from potentates to American ambassadors are laid up here: gold snuff-boxes set in diamonds, and a glittering array of swords and scymitars. There was one fine Damascus blade; but it seemed too blunt to do any harm.—Then we lost ourselves in a large collection of medals and coins,—Roman gold coins, with fat old Vespasian and others; from which we were recalled to find ourselves in the extremely modern and democratic United States! It was a very interesting morning.

We took advantage of a mild day to ascend to the
skylight of the dome of the Capitol, in order to obtain
a view of the surrounding country.   The ascent was
rather fatiguing, but perfectly safe.   The residents
at Washington declare the environs to be beautiful
in all seasons but early winter; the meadows being
gay with a profusion of wild flowers; even as early
as February with several kinds of heartsease.   It
was a particularly cold season when I was there;
but on the day of my departure, in the middle of
February, the streets were one sheet of ice; and I
remember we made a long slide from the steps of
our boarding-house to those of the stage.   But I
believe that that winter was no rule for others.—
From the summit of the Capitol, we saw plainly
marked out the basin in which Washington stands,
surrounded by hills, except where the Potomac
spreads its waters.   The city was intended to
occupy the whole of this basin, and its seven
theoretical avenues may be traced; but all except
Pennsylvania Avenue are bare and forlorn.   A few
mean houses dotted about, the sheds of a navy-yard
on one bank of the Potomac, and three or four
villas on the other, are all the objects that relieve
the eye in this space intended to be so busy and
magnificent.   The city is a grand mistake.   Its
only attraction is its being the seat of government;
and it is thought that it will not long continue to

be so.   The far-western States begin to demand a
more central seat for Congress; and the Cincinnati
people are already speculating upon which of their
hills or table-lands is to be the site of the new
Capitol.   Whenever this change takes place, all
will be over with Washington: "thorns shall come
up in her palaces, and the owl and the raven shall
dwell in it," while her sister cities of the east will
be still spreading as fast as hands can be found to
build them.

There was a funeral of a member of Congress
on the 30th of January;—the interment of the
representative from South Carolina whose death I
mentioned in connexion with Mr. Calhoun.   We
were glad that we were at Washington at the time,
as a congressional funeral is a remarkable spectacle.
We went to the Capitol at about half an hour
before noon, and found many ladies already seated
in the gallery of the Hall of Representatives.   I
chanced to be placed at the precise point of the
gallery where the sounds from every part of the
house are concentred; so that I heard the whole
service, while I was at such a distance as to command
a view of the entire scene.   In the chair were the
President of the Senate and the Speaker of the
Representatives.   Below them sat the officiating
clergyman; immediately opposite to whom were the
President and the Heads of Departments on one

side the coffin, and the Judges of the Supreme
Court and members of the Senate on the other.
The Representatives sat in rows behind, each with
crape round the left arm; some in black; many in
blue coats with bright buttons. Some of the
fiercest political foes in the country,— some who
never meet on any other occasion,—the President
and the South Carolina senators, for instance,—
now sat knee to knee, necessarily looking into each
others' faces. With a coffin beside them, and such
an event awaiting their exit, how out of place was
hatred here!

After prayers, there was a sermon, in which
warning of death was brought home to all, and
particularly to the aged; and the vanity of all
disturbances of human passion when in view of the
grave was dwelt upon. There sat the grey-headed
old President, at that time feeble, and looking
scarcely able to go through this ceremonial. I saw
him apparently listening to the discourse; I saw
him rise when it was over, and follow the coffin in
his turn, somewhat feebly; I saw him disappear in
the doorway; and immediately descended with my
party to the Rotundo, in order to witness the
departure of the procession for the grave. At the
bottom of the stairs, a member of Congress met
us, pale and trembling, with the news that the
President had been twice fired at with a pistol, by

an assassin who had waylaid him in the portico;
but that both pistols had missed fire. At this
moment the assassin rushed into the Rotundo where
we were standing, pursued, and instantly surrounded
by a crowd. I saw his hands and half-bare arms
struggling above the heads of the crowd, in resist-
ance to being handcuffed. He was presently over-
powered, conveyed to a carriage, and taken before
a magistrate. The attack threw the old soldier into
a tremendous passion. He fears nothing; but his
temper is not equal to his courage. Instead of his
putting the event calmly aside, and proceeding with
the business of the hour, it was found necessary to
put him into his carriage and take him home.

We feared what the consequences would be.
We had little doubt that the assassin Lawrence was
mad; and as little that before the day was out, we
should hear the crime imputed to more than
one political party or individual. And so it was.
Before two hours were over, the name of almost
every eminent politician was mixed up with that of
the poor maniac who caused the uproar. The
President's misconduct on the occasion was the
most virulent and protracted. A deadly enmity
had long subsisted between General Jackson and
Mr. Poindexter, a senator of the United States,
which had been much aggravated since General
Jackson's accession by some unwarrantable language

which he had publicly used in relation to Mr.
Poindexter's private affairs. There was a prevalent
expectation of a duel, as soon as the expiration of
the President's term of office should enable his
foe to send him a challenge. Under these circumstances, the President thought proper to charge
Mr. Poindexter with being the instigator of Lawrence's attempt. He did this in conversation so
frequently and openly, that Mr. Poindexter wrote a
letter, brief and manly, stating that he understood
this charge was made against him, but that he
would not believe it till it was confirmed by the
President himself; his not replying to this letter
being understood to be such a confirmation. The
President showed this letter to visitors at the White
House, and did not answer it. He went further;
obtaining affidavits (tending to implicate Poindexter)
from weak and vile persons whose evidence utterly
failed; having personal interviews with these creatures, and openly showing a disposition to hunt his
foe to destruction at all hazards. The issue was
that Lawrence was proved to have acted from sheer
insanity; Poindexter made a sort of triumphal
progress through the States; and an irretrievable
stain was left upon President Jackson's name.

Every one was anxiously anticipating the fierce
meeting of these foes, on the President's retirement
from office, when Mr. Poindexter, last year, in a fit

either of somnambulism, or of delirium from illness, walked out of a chamber window in the middle of the night, and was so much injured that he soon died.

It so happened that we were engaged to a party at Mr. Poindexter's the very evening of this attack upon the President. There was so tremendous a thunder-storm, that our host and hostess were disappointed of almost all their guests except ourselves; and we had difficulty in merely crossing the street, being obliged to have planks laid across the flood which gushed between the carriage and the steps of the door. The conversation naturally turned on the event of the morning. I knew little of the quarrel which was now to be so dreadfully aggravated; but the more I afterwards heard, the more I admired the moderation with which Mr. Poindexter spoke of his foe that night, and as often as I subsequently met him.

I had intended to visit the President the day after the funeral; but I heard so much of his determination to consider the attack a political affair, and I had so little wish to hear it thus treated, against the better knowledge of all the world, that I stayed away as long as I could. Before I went, I was positively assured of Lawrence's insanity by one of the physicians who were appointed to visit him. One of the poor creature's complaints was, that General Jackson deprived him of the British crown, to which he was heir.   When I did go to the White House, I took the briefest possible notice to the President of the "insane attempt" of Lawrence : but the word roused his ire. *He protested, in the presence of many strangers, that there was no insanity in the case.   I was silent, of course. He protested that there was a plot, and that the man was a tool, and at length quoted the Attorney-General as his authority.   It was painful to hear a Chief Ruler publicly trying to persuade a foreigner that any of his constituents hated him to the death : and I took the liberty of changing the subject as soon as I could.   The next evening I was at the Attorney-General's, and I asked him how he could let himself be quoted as saying that Lawrence was not mad.   He excused himself by saying that he meant general insanity.   He believed Lawrence insane in one direction,—that it was a sort of Ravaillac case.   I besought him to impress the President with this view of the case as soon as might be.

It would be amusing, if it were possible, to furnish a complete set of the rumours, injurious (if they had not been too absurd) to all parties in turn, upon this single and very common act of a madman. One would have thought that no maniac had ever before attacked a Chief Magistrate.   The act might so easily have remained fruitless! but it was made to bear a full and poisonous crop of folly, wickedness, and woe. I feared on the instant how it would be, and felt that, though the President was safe, it was very bad news. When will it come to be thought possible for politicians to have faith in one another, though they may differ, and to be jealous for their rivals rather than for themselves?

THE CAPITOL.

" . . You have unto the support of a true and natural aristocracy the deepest root of a democracy that hath been planted.
Wherefore there is nothing in art or nature better qualified for the
result than this assembly."

Harrington's Oceana.

THE places of resort for the stranger in the Capitol
are the Library, the Supreme Court, the Senate
Chamber, and the Hall of Representatives.

The former Library of Congress was burnt by
the British in their atrocious attack upon Washington in 1814. Jefferson then offered his, and it was
purchased by the nation. It is perpetually increased
by annual appropriations. We did not go to the
Library to read, but amused ourselves for many
pleasant hours with the prints, and with the fine
medals which we found there. I was never tired
of the cabinet of Napoleon medals; the most beautifully composed piece of history that I ever studied.
There is a cup carved by Benvenuto Cellini,
preserved among the curiosities of the Capitol,
which might be studied for a week before all the
mysteries of its design are apprehended. How it
found its way to so remote a resting-place, I do not
remember.

Judge Story was kind enough to send us notice when any cause was to be argued in the Supreme Court which it was probable we might be able to understand; and we passed a few mornings there. The apartment is less fitted for its purposes than any other in the building; the court being badly lighted and ventilated. The windows are at the back of the Judges, whose countenances are therefore indistinctly seen, and who sit in their own light. Visitors are usually placed behind the counsel and opposite the Judges, or on seats on each side. I was kindly offered the reporter's chair, in a snug corner, under the Judges, and facing the counsel; and there I was able to hear much of the pleading, and to see the remarkable countenances of the Attorney-General, Clay, Webster, Porter, and others, in the fullest light that could be had in this dim chamber.

At some moments this court presents a singular spectacle. I have watched the assemblage while the Chief Justice was delivering a judgment;—the three Judges on either hand gazing at him, more like learners than associates;—Webster standing firm as a rock, his large, deep-set eyes wide awake, his lips compressed, and his whole countenance in that intent stillness which instantly fixes the eye of the stranger;—Clay leaning against the desk in an attitude whose grace contrasts strangely with the

slovenly make of his dress, his snuff-box for the
moment unopened in his hand, his small grey eye
and placid half-smile conveying an expression of
pleasure which redeems his face from its usual
unaccountable commonness;—the Attorney-General, his fingers playing among his papers, his quick
black eye, and thin tremulous lips for once fixed,
his small face, pale with thought, contrasting remarkably with the other two;—these men, absorbed
in what they are listening to, thinking neither of
themselves, nor of each other, while they are
watched by the groups of idlers and listeners around
them,—the newspaper corps, the dark Cherokee
chiefs, the stragglers from the far west, the gay
ladies in their waving plumes, and the members of
either house that have stepped in to listen,—all
these have I seen at one moment constitute one
silent assemblage, while the mild voice of the
aged Chief-Justice sounded through the Court.

Every one is aware that the wigs and gowns of
counsel are not to be seen in the United States.
There was no knowing, when Webster sauntered
in, threw himself down, and leaned back against
the table, his dreamy eyes seeming to see nothing
about him, whether he would by-and-by take up
his hat, and go away, or whether he would rouse
himself suddenly, and stand up to address the
Judges. For the generality there was no knowing;

and to us, who were forewarned, it was amusing to
see how the Court would fill after the entrance of
Webster, and empty when he had gone back to the
Senate Chamber. The chief interest to me in
Webster's pleading, and also in his speaking in the
Senate, was from seeing one so dreamy and *nonchalant* roused into strong excitement. It seemed like
having a curtain lifted up, through which it was impossible to pry ; like hearing autobiographical secrets.
Webster is a lover of ease and pleasure, and has
an air of the most unaffected indolence and careless
self-sufficiency. It is something to see him moved
with anxiety and the toil of intellectual conflict : to
see his lips tremble, his nostrils expand, the perspi-
ration start upon his brow ; to hear his voice vary
with emotion, and to watch the expression of labo-
rious thought while he pauses, for minutes together,
to consider his notes, and decide upon the arrangement of his argument. These are the moments
when it becomes clear that this pleasure-loving man
works for his honours and his gains. He seems to
have the desire which other remarkable men have
shown, to conceal the extent of his toils ; and his
wish has been favoured by some accidents,—some
sudden, unexpected call upon him for a display of
knowledge and power which has electrified the
beholders. But on such occasions he has been able
to bring into use acquisitions and exercises intended

for other occasions, on which they may or may not
have been wanted.   No one will suppose that this
is said in disparagement of Mr. Webster.   It is only
saying that he owes to his own industry what he
must otherwise owe to miracle.

What his capacity for toil is was shown, in one
instance among many, in an affair of great interest
to his own State.   On the 7th of April, 1830, the
town of Salem, Massachusetts, was thrown into a
state of consternation by the announcement of a
horrible murder.   Mr. White, a respectable and
wealthy citizen of Salem, about eighty years of age,
was found murdered in his bed.   The circumstances were such as to indicate that the murder
was not for common purposes of plunder ; and suspicions arose which made every citizen shudder at
the idea of the community in which he lived containing the monsters who would perpetrate such a
deed.   A patrol of the citizens was proposed and
organized, and none were more zealous in propositions and in patrolling than   Joseph and John
Knapp, relatives of the murdered man.   The conduct of these young men on the occasion exposed
them to dislike before any one breathed suspicion.
Several acquaintances of the family paid visits of
condolence before the funeral.   One of these told me,
still with a feeling of horror, how one of the Knapps
pulled his sleeve, and asked in an awkward whisper,

whether he would go up stairs and see " the old devil." The old gentleman's housekeeper had slept out of the house that particular night; a back window had been left unfastened, with a plank placed against it on the outside ; and a will of the old gentleman's (happily a superseded one) was missing. Suspicious circumstances like these were found soon to have accumulated so as to justify the arrest of the two Knapps, and of two brothers of the name of Crowninshield. A lawyer was ready with testimony that Joseph Knapp, who had married a grand-niece of Mr. White, had obtained legal information that if Mr. White died intestate, Knapp's mother-in-law would succeed to half the property. Joseph Knapp confessed the whole in prison, and Richard Crowninshield, doubtless the principal assassin, destroyed himself. The State prosecutors were in a great difficulty. Without the confession, the evidence was scarcely sufficient ; and though Joseph Knapp was promised favour from Government if he would repeat his evidence on the side of the prosecution in court, it was not safe, as the event proved, to rely upon this in a case otherwise doubtful. The Attorney and Solicitor-General of the State were both aged and feeble men; and as the day of trial drew on, it became more and more doubtful whether they would be equal to the occasion, and whether these ruffians, well understood

to be the murderers, would not be let loose upon
society again, from bad management of the prosecution.   The prosecuting officers of the Government
were prevailed upon, within three days of the trial,
to send to seek out Mr. Webster, and request his
assistance.

A citizen of Salem, a friend of mine, was deputed to carry the request.   He went to Boston : Mr.
Webster was not there, but at his farm by the
sea-shore.   Thither, in tremendous weather, my
friend followed him.   Mr. Webster was playing che-
quers with his boy.   The old farmer sat by the fire,
his wife and two young women were sewing and
knitting coarse stockings ; one of these last, however, being no farmer's daughter, but Mr. Webster's
bride ; for this was shortly after his second marriage.
My friend was first dried and refreshed, and then
lost no time in mentioning " business."   Mr.
Webster writhed at the word, saying that he came
down hither to get out of hearing of it.   He next
declared that his undertaking anything more was
entirely out of the question, and pointed, in evidence,
to his swollen bag of briefs lying in a corner.
However, upon a little further explanation and
meditation, he agreed to the request with the same
good grace with which he afterwards went through
with his task.   He made himself master of all that
my friend could communicate, and before daybreak

was off through the woods, in the unabated storm,— no doubt meditating his speech by the way. He needed all the assistance that could be given him, of course : and my friend constituted himself Mr. Webster's fetcher and carrier of facts for these two days. He says he was never under orders before since his childish days ; but in this emergency he was a willing servant, obeying such laconic instructions as " Go there ;" " Learn this and that ;" " Now go away ;" and so forth.

At the appointed hour, Mr. Webster was completely ready. His argument is thought one of the finest, in every respect, that he has produced. I read it before I knew anything of the circumstances which I have related ; and I was made acquainted with them in consequence of my inquiry how a man could be hanged on evidence so apparently insufficient as that adduced by the prosecution. Mr. Webster had made all that could be made of it ; his argument was ingenious and close, and imbued with moral beauty ; but the fact was, as I was assured, the prisoners were convicted on the ground of the confession of the criminal, more than on the evidence adduced by the prosecutors ; though the confession could not, after all, be made open use of. The prisoners had such an opinion of the weakness of the case, that Joseph, who had been offered favour by Government, refused to testify, and the pledge of the

Government was withdrawn. Both the Knapps were hanged.

The clearness with which, in this case, a multitude of minute facts is arranged, and the ingenuity with which a long chain of circumstantial evidence is drawn out, can be understood only through a reading of the entire argument. Even these are less remarkable than the sympathy by which the pleader seems to have possessed himself of the emotions, the peculiar moral experience, of the quiet good people of Salem, when thunderstruck with this event. While shut up at his task, Mr. Webster found means to see into the hearts which were throbbing in all the homes about him. " One thing more," said he to my friend, who was taking his leave of him on the eve of the trial. " Do you know of anything remarkable about any of the jury?" My friend had nothing to say, unless it was that the foreman was a man of a remarkably tender conscience. To this we doubtless owe the concluding passage of the argument, delivered, as I was told, in a voice and manner less solemn than easy and tranquil.

" Gentlemen,—Your whole concern should be to do your duty, and leave consequences to take care of themselves. You will receive the law from the Court. Your verdict, it is true, may endanger the prisoner's life; but then it is to save other lives.

If the prisoner's guilt has been shown and proved, beyond all reasonable doubt, you will convict him. If such reasonable doubts still remain, you will acquit him. You are the judges of the whole case. You owe a duty to the public, as well as to the prisoner at the bar. You cannot presume to be wiser than the law. Your duty is a plain, straight-forward one. Doubtless, we would all judge him in mercy. Towards him, as an individual, the law inculcates no hostility ;—but towards him, if proved to be a murderer, the law, and the oaths you have taken, and public justice, demand that you do your duty.

" With consciences satisfied with the discharge of duty, no consequences can harm you. There is no evil that we cannot face or fly from, but the consciousness of duty disregarded.

" A sense of duty pursues us ever. It is omnipresent, like the Deity. If we take to ourselves the wings of the morning, and dwell in the uttermost parts of the seas, duty performed, or duty violated, is still with us, for our happiness or our misery. If we say the darkness shall cover us, in the darkness as in the light, our obligations are yet with us. We cannot escape their power, nor fly from their presence. They are with us in this life, will be with us at its close ; and in that scene of inconceivable solemnity, which lies yet farther onward, we shall still find ourselves surrounded by the consciousness of duty, to pain us wherever it has been violated, and to console us, so far as God may have given us grace to perform it."

How must the mention of the tremendous " secret" have thrilled through the hearts of citizens who had for weeks been anxiously searching every man's countenance to find it out.   The picture given as from the pleader's imagination, was, as every man knew, derived from the confession of the criminal.

" The deed was executed with a degree of self-possession and steadiness, equal to the wickedness with which it was planned.   The circumstances, now clearly in evidence, spread out the whole scene before us.   Deep sleep had fallen on the destined victim, and on all beneath his roof.   A healthful old man, to whom sleep was sweet, the first sound slumbers of the night held in their soft but strong embrace.   The assassin enters, through the window already prepared, into an unoccupied apartment. With noiseless foot he paces the lonely hall, half lighted by the moon ; he winds up the ascent of the stairs, and reaches the door of the chamber.   Of this he moves the lock, by soft and continued pressure, till it turns on its hinges, and he enters, and beholds his victim before him.   The room was uncommonly open to the admission of light.   The face of the innocent sleeper was turned from the murderer, and the beams of the moon, resting on the grey locks of his aged temple, showed him where to strike. The fatal blow is given! and the victim passes, without a struggle or a motion, from the repose of sleep to the repose of death! It is the assassin's purpose to make sure work; and he yet plies the dagger, though it was obvious that life had been destroyed by the blow of the bludgeon. He even raises the aged arm, that he may not fail in his aim at the heart, and replaces it again over the wounds of the poniard. To finish the picture, he explores the wrist for the pulse! he feels it, and ascertains that it beats no longer! It is accomplished. The deed is done. He retreats, retraces his steps to the window, passes out through it as he came in, and escapes. He has done the murder,— no eye has seen him, no ear has heard him. The *secret* is his own, and it is safe! Ah, gentlemen, that was a dreadful mistake. Such a secret can be safe nowhere. The whole creation of God has neither nook nor corner, where the guilty can bestow it, and say it is safe. Not to speak of that Eye which glances through all disguises, and beholds everything, as in the splendour of noon,—such secrets of guilt are never safe from detection, even by men. True it is, generally speaking, that 'murder will out.' True it is, that Providence hath so

ordained, and doth so govern things, that those who
break the great law of heaven by shedding man's
blood, seldom succeed in avoiding discovery. Especially, in a case exciting so much attention as this,
discovery must come, and will come, sooner or later.
A thousand eyes turn at once to explore every man,
every thing, every circumstance, connected with the
time and place : a thousand ears catch every whisper, a thousand excited minds intensely dwell on the
scene, shedding all their light, and ready to kindle
the slightest circumstance into a blaze of discovery.
Meantime, the guilty soul cannot keep its own secret. It is false to itself; or rather it feels an irresistible impulse of conscience to be true to itself.
It labours under its guilty possession, and knows
not what to do with it. The human heart was not
made for the residence of such an inhabitant. It
finds itself preyed on by a torment, which it does
not acknowledge to God or man. A vulture is
devouring it, and it can ask no sympathy or assistance, either from heaven or earth. The secret
which the murderer possesses soon comes to possess
him ; and like the evil spirits of which we read, it
overcomes him, and leads him whithersoever it will.
He feels it beating at his heart, rising to his throat,
and demanding disclosure. He thinks the whole
world sees it in his face, reads it in his eyes, and
almost hears its workings in the very silence of his

thoughts. It has become his master. It betrays his discretion, it breaks down his courage, it conquers his prudence. When suspicions from without begin to embarrass him, and the net of circumstance to entangle him, the fatal *secret* struggles with still greater violence to burst forth. It must be confessed: *it will be* confessed; there is no refuge from confession but suicide; and suicide is confession."

Mr. Webster was born in 1782, in New Hampshire. His father was a farmer who had retreated into the wilderness, and, as his son says, " had lighted his fire nearer to the North Pole than any other citizen of the States." The good man had, however, come down into the meadows at the foot of the hills before his second son Daniel was born. By the means which are within reach of almost every child in his country,—the schools and colleges of easy access,—Daniel became qualified for an apprenticeship to law; and by industry, great intellectual power, and some few fortunate accidents, rose into notice, employment, and eminence. He has for some years been considered the head of the federal party; and he is therefore now on the losing side in politics. His last great triumph was his exposure of the Nullification doctrine, in 1833. Since that time, he has maintained his influence in Congress by virtue of his great talents and former services; but, his politics being in opposition to those of the great body of the people, he is unable to do more than head the opposition in the Senate. He was an unsuccessful candidate in the last Presidential election; and there seems little probability of his attainment of office, unless by his taking the lead of the abolition movement. For this it is probably now too late. The abolitionists have done the most difficult part of their work, in rousing the public mind: they are chiefly of the democratic side in politics; and they do not entertain, I believe, that faith in the great leader of the federalists, which would induce them to support his claims as the anti-slavery candidate for the next Presidentship.

Mr. Webster owes his rise to the institutions under which he lives,—institutions which open the race to the swift, and the battle to the strong; but there is little in him that is congenial with them. He is aristocratic in his tastes and habits: and but little republican simplicity is to be recognized in him. Neither his private conversation nor his public transactions usually convey an impression that he is in earnest. When he is so, his power is majestic, irresistible; but his ambition for office, and for the good opinion of those who surround him, is seen too often in alternation with his love of ease and luxury, to allow of his being confided in as he is admired. If it had been otherwise, if his moral had equalled his intellectual supremacy, if his aims had been as single as his reason is unclouded, he would long ago have carried all before him, and been the virtual monarch of the United States. But to have expected this would have been unreasonable. The very best men of any society are rarely or never to be found among its eminent statesmen; and it is not fair to look for them in offices which, in the present condition of human affairs, would yield to such no other choice than of speedy failure or protracted martyrdom. Taking great politicians as they are, Mr. Webster's general consistency may be found not to have fallen below the average, though it has not been so remarkable as to ensure on his behalf a confidence at all to be compared with the universal admiration of his talents.

Mr. Webster speaks seldom in the Senate. When he does, it is generally on some constitutional question, where his reasoning powers and knowledge are brought into play, and where his authority is considered so high, that he has the glorious satisfaction of knowing that he is listened to as an oracle by an assemblage of the first men in the country. Previous to such an exercise, he may be seen leaning back in his chair, not, as usual, biting the top of his pen, or twirling his thumbs, or bursting into sudden and transient laughter at Colonel Benton's oratorical absurdities, but absent and thoughtful, making notes, and seeing nothing that is before his eyes. When he rises, his voice is moderate, and his manner quiet, with the slightest possible mixture of embarrassment; his right hand rests upon his desk, and the left hangs by his side. Before his first head is finished, however, his voice has risen so as to fill the chamber and ring again, and he has fallen into his favourite attitude, with his left hand under his coat-tail, and the right in full action. At this moment, the eye rests upon him as upon one under the true inspiration of seeing the invisible, and grasping the impalpable. When the vision has passed away, the change is astonishing. He sits at his desk, writing letters or dreaming, so that he does not always discover when the Senate is going to a division. Some one of his party has not seldom to jog his elbow, and tell him that his vote is wanted.

There can scarcely be a stronger contrast than between the eloquence of Webster and that of Clay. Mr. Clay is now my personal friend; but I have a distinct recollection of my impressions of his speaking, while he was yet merely an acquaintance. His appearance is plain in the extreme, being that of a mere west-country farmer. He is tall and thin, with a weather-beaten complexion, small grey eyes, which convey an idea of something more than his well-known sagacity,—even of slyness. It is only after much intercourse that Mr. Clay's personal appearance can be discovered to do him any justice at all. All attempts to take his likeness have been in vain, though upwards of thirty portraits of him, by different artists, were in existence when I was in America. No one has succeeded in catching the subtle expression of placid kindness, mingled with astuteness, which becomes visible to the eyes of those who are in daily intercourse with him. His mode of talking, deliberate and somewhat formal, including sometimes a grave humour, and sometimes a gentle sentiment, very touching from the lips of a sagacious man of ambition, has but one fault,—its obvious adaptation to the supposed state of mind of the person to whom it is addressed. Mr. Clay is a man of an irritable and impetuous nature, over which he has obtained a truly noble mastery. His moderation is now his most striking characteristic; obtained, no doubt, at the cost of prodigious self-denial, on his own part, and on that of his friends, of some of the ease, naturalness, and self-forgetfulness of his manners and discourse. But his conversation is rich in information, and full charged with the spirit of justice and kindliness, rising, on occasion, to a moving magnanimity. By chances, of some of which he was totally unaware, I became acquainted with several acts of his life, political and private, which prove that his moderation is not the mere diffusion of oil upon the waves, but the true stilling of the storm of passion and selfishness. The time may come when these acts may be told; but it has not yet arrived.

Mr. Clay is sometimes spoken of as a " disappointed statesman," and he would probably not object to call himself so ; for it makes no part of his idea of dignity to pretend to be satisfied when he is sorry, or delighted with what he would fain have prevented : but he suffers only the genuine force of disappointment, without the personal mortification and loss of dignity which are commonly supposed to be included in it. He once held the balance of the Union in his hand, and now belongs to the losing party : he more than once expected to be President, and has now no chance of ever being so. Thus far he is a disappointed statesman ; but at the same time, he is in possession of more than an equivalent for what he has lost—not only in the disciplined moderation of his temper, but in the imperishable reality of great deeds done. No possession of office could now add to his dignity, any more than the total neglect of the present generation of the people could detract from it. The fact that Mr. Clay's political opinions are not in accordance with those now held by the great body of the people, is no disgrace to him or them ; while the dignity of his former services, supported by his present patience and quietness, places him far above compassion, and every feeling but respect and admiration. This admiration is exalted to enthusiasm in those who know how difficult it is to a man of Mr. Clay's nature, who has lived in public all his life, to fall back into obscurity,—an obscurity not relieved, alas! by the solace of a cheerful home. Few spectacles can be more noble than he is in that obscurity, discoursing of public men and affairs with a justice which no rivalship can impair, and a hopefulness which no personal disappointment can relax.

Mr. Clay is the son of a respectable clergyman in Virginia, and was born in April, 1777. His father died when he was quite young; and he was in consequence left to the common educational chances which befriend all the young citizens of the United States. He studied law, after leaving the common school at which his education began, and settled early at Lexington, in Kentucky, where his residence has ever since been fixed. His first important act was labouring diligently in favour of a plan for the gradual abolition of slavery in Kentucky, which was proposed in 1798. His exertions were, however, in vain. In 1803, he entered the legislature of his State, and in 1806 was sent, with the dignity of senator, to Washington, having not quite attained the requisite age. In 1809, he found occasion to advocate the principle of protection to domestic manufactures which he has since had the very questionable honour of embodying in his famous American System.   In 1811, he became Speaker of the House of Representatives, and for three years exercised in that situation a powerful influence over the affairs of the country.   In 1814, he was appointed one of the Commissioners who negociated the treaty of Ghent; and when that business was concluded, he repaired to London, with his colleagues, Messrs. Adams and Gallatin, and there concluded the commercial convention which was made the basis of all the subsequent commercial arrangements between the United States and Europe.   In 1825, Mr. Clay accepted the appointment of Secretary of State under Mr. Adams, an act for which he is still extensively and vehemently blamed, but with how much or how little reason, I do not pretend, from want of knowledge of the party politics of the time, to understand.   While in this office, he did a great deal in procuring, with much labour and difficulty, a recognition of the independence of the Spanish colonies in South America; a recognition which had the all-important effect of deterring the great European powers from their contemplated intervention on behalf of Spain.   Mr. Clay's speeches were read at the head of the armies of the South American republics; and if his name were forgotten everywhere else, it would stand in the history of their independence.

Mr. Clay has since been a powerful advocate of internal improvements, and the framer of "the American System,"—the founder of the protective policy, which I believe he is more proud of than of any act of his public life, while many others are justly amazed that a man of his sagacity should not see the unsoundness of the principle on which the whole system is based. Much more honour is due to him for the Compromise Bill, by which he virtually surrendered his system, and immediately put an end to the Nullification struggle. Mr. Webster victoriously exposed the badness of the Nullification principle; and Mr. Clay removed the present cause of its exercise. The one humbled South Carolina to the dust on her Nullification ground; the other left her in triumphant possession of her principle of Free Trade, while disarming her by a wise and well-principled compromise.

The one act of Mr. Clay's public life, for which he must be held to require pardon from posterity, is that by which he secured the continuance of slavery in Missouri; and, in consequence, its establishment in Arkansas and Florida,—the one an admitted State, the other a Territory destined to be so. Mr. Clay is not an advocate of Slavery, though, instead of being a friend to Abolition, he is a dupe to Colonization. When he held the destinies of American Slavery in his hand, he had unhappily

more regard for precedent in human arrangements
than for the spirit of the divine laws in the light of
which such arrangements should be ever regarded.
He acted to avert the conflict which cannot be
averted. It has still to take place,—it is now taking
place,—under less favourable circumstances; and
his measure of expediency is already meeting with
the retribution which ever follows upon the subordination of a higher principle to a lower. For
many of his public acts, Mr. Clay will be perma-
nently honoured; with regard to others, the honour
will be mingled with allowance for error in philosophy; for this one he will have to be forgiven.

Mr. Clay married an excellent woman, who is
still living, the survivor of six daughters, taken away,
some of them in the bloom of promise, and one in
the maturity of virtue. The great statesman's house
is very desolate. He must seek in his own strength
of soul, and in the love and honour with which his
friends regard him, that good which has been denied
to him in the latter days of his political and domestic
life.

His recollections of Europe are very vivid and
pleasurable. We spent many an hour of my visit
to him in Kentucky in talking over our mutual
English friends, till we forgot the time and space
we had both traversed since we parted from them,
and looked up surprised to find ourselves, not

at a London dinner-table, but in the wild woods of the west. Mr. Clay has not kept up his knowledge of British life and politics so accurately as some of his brother-statesmen; but he is still full of the sayings of Castlereagh and Canning, of Lords Eldon and Stowell, of Mackintosh and Sydney Smith.

The finest speech I heard from Mr. Clay in the Senate was on the sad subject of the injuries of the Indians. He exposed the facts of the treatment of the Cherokees by Georgia. He told how the lands in Georgia, guaranteed by solemn treaties to the Cherokees, had been surveyed and partitioned off to white citizens of the State; that, though there is a nominal right of appeal awarded to the complainants, this is a mere mockery, as an acknowledgment of the right of Georgia to divide the lands is made a necessary preliminary to the exercise of the right: —in other words, the Indians must lay down their claims on the threshold of the courts which they enter for the purpose of enforcing these claims! The object of Mr. Clay's plea was to have the Supreme Court open to the Cherokees, their case being, he contended, contemplated by the Constitution. A minor proposition was that Congress should assist, with territory and appliances, a body of Cherokees who desired to emigrate beyond the Mississippi.

It was known that Mr. Clay would probably

bring forward his great topic that day. Some of the foreign ambassadors might be seen leaning against the pillars behind the chair; and many members of the other House appeared behind, and in the passages: and one sat on the steps of the platform, his hands clasped, and his eyes fixed on Mr. Clay, as if life hung upon his words. As many as could crowd into the gallery leaned over the balustrade; and the lower circle was thronged with ladies and gentlemen, in the centre of whom stood a group of Cherokee chiefs, listening immoveably. I never saw so deep a moral impression produced by a speech. The best testimony to this was the general disgust excited by the empty and abusive reply of the senator from Georgia,—who, by the way, might be judged from his accent to have been about three months from the Green Island. This gentleman's speech, however, showed us one good thing,—that Mr. Clay is as excellent in reply as in proposition; —prompt, earnest, temperate, and graceful. The chief characteristic of his eloquence is its earnestness. Every tone of his voice, every fibre of his frame bears testimony to this. His attitudes are, from the beginning to the close, very graceful. His first sentences are homely, and given with a little hesitation and repetition, and with an agitation shown by a frequent putting on and taking off of the spectacles, and a trembling of the hands among the documents on the desk. Then as the speaker becomes possessed with his subject, the agitation changes its character, but does not subside. His utterance is still deliberate, but his voice becomes deliciously winning. Its higher tones disappointed me at first; but the lower ones, trembling with emotion, swelling and falling with the earnestness of the speaker, are very moving; and his whole manner becomes irresistibly persuasive. I saw tears, of which I am sure he was wholly unconscious, falling on his papers, as he vividly described the woes and injuries of the aborigines. I saw Webster draw his hand across his eyes; I saw every one deeply moved except two persons,—the Vice-president, who yawned somewhat ostentatiously, and the Georgian senator, who was busy brewing his storm. I was amazed at the daring of this gentleman,—at the audacity which could break up such a moral impression as this Cherokee tale, so told, had produced, by accusing Mr. Clay of securing an interest in opposition to Georgia " by stage starts and theatric gesticulations." The audience were visibly displeased at having their feelings thus treated, in the presence even of the Cherokee chiefs: but Mr. Clay's replies both to argument and abuse were so happy, and the Georgian's rejoinder was so outrageous, that the business ended with a general burst of laughter. The propositions were to lie over till the next day; and, as I soon after left Washington, I never learned their ultimate fate.

The American Senate is a most imposing assemblage. When I first entered it, I thought I never saw a finer set of heads than the forty-six before my eyes:—two only being absent, and the Union then consisting of twenty-four States. Mr. Calhoun's countenance first fixed my attention; the splendid eye, the straight forehead, surmounted by a load of stiff, upright, dark hair; the stern brow; the inflexible mouth;—it is one of the most remarkable heads in the country. Next him sat his colleague, Mr. Preston, in singular contrast,—stout in person, with a round, ruddy, good-humoured face, large blue eyes, and a wig, orange to-day, brown yesterday, and golden to-morrow. Near them sat Colonel Benton, a temporary people's man, remarkable chiefly for his pomposity. He sat swelling amidst his piles of papers and books, looking like a being designed by nature to be a good-humoured barber or innkeeper, but forced by fate to make himself into a mock-heroic senator. Opposite sat the transcendant Webster, with his square forehead and cavernous eyes: and behind him the homely Clay, with the face and figure of a farmer, but something of the air of a divine, from his hair being combed straight back from his temples. Near them

sat Southard and Porter; the former astute and
rapid in countenance and gesture ; the latter
strangely mingling a boyish fun and lightness of
manner and glance with the sobriety suitable to the
Judge and the Senator. His keen eye takes in
every thing that passes; his extraordinary mouth,
with its overhanging upper lip, has but to unfold
into a smile to win laughter from the sourest official
or demagogue. Then there was the bright *bonhommie* of Ewing of Ohio, the most primitive-
looking of senators ; and the benign, religious
gravity of Frelinghuysen; the gentlemanly air of
Buchanan; the shrewdness of Poindexter; the
somewhat melancholy simplicity of Silsbee,—all
these, and many others were striking ; and for
nothing more than for their total unlikeness to each
other. No English person who has not travelled
over half the world, can form an idea of such
differences among men forming one assembly for
the same purposes, and speaking the same language.
Some were descended from Dutch farmers, some
from French huguenots, some from Scotch puritans,
some from English cavaliers, some from Irish
chieftains. They were brought together out of law-
courts, sugar-fields, merchants' stores, mountain-
farms, forests and prairies. The stamp of originality
was impressed on every one, and inspired a deep,
involuntary respect. I have seen no assembly of

chosen men, and no company of the high-born,
invested with the antique dignities of an antique
realm, half so imposing to the imagination as this
collection of stout-souled, full-grown, original men,
brought together on the ground of their supposed
sufficiency, to work out the will of their diverse
constituencies.

In this splendid chamber, thus splendidly inhabited, we spent many hours of many weeks.   Here
I was able to gain no little knowledge of the state,
political and other, of various parts of the country,
from my large acquaintance among the members of
the Senate.   When dull official reports were read,
and uninteresting local matters were discussed, or
when the one interminable speaker, Benton, was on
his legs, one member or another of the body would
come and talk with us.   I have heard certain of
the members, stalking from their seats towards
those of the ladies, compared to cranes in search of
fish.   The comparison is not a bad one.

I wished, every day, that the ladies would conduct
themselves in a more dignified manner than they
did, in the Senate.   They came in with waving
plumes, and glittering in all the colours of the
rainbow, causing no little bustle in the place, no
little annoyance to the gentlemen spectators; and
rarely sat still for any length of time.   I know that
these ladies are no fair specimen of the women who

would attend parliamentary proceedings in any other metropolis. I know that they were the wives, daughters and sisters of legislators, women thronging to Washington for purposes of convenience or pleasure, leaving their usual employments behind them, and seeking to pass away the time. I knew this, and made allowance accordingly; but I still wished that they could understand the gravity of such an assembly, and show so much respect to it as to repay the privilege of admission by striving to excite as little attention as possible, and by having the patience to sit still when they happened not to be amused, till some interruption gave them opportunity to depart quietly. If they had done this, Judge Porter would not have moved that they should be appointed seats in the gallery instead of below; and they would have been guiltless of furnishing a plea for the exclusion of women, who would probably make a better use of the privilege, from the galleries of other houses of parliament.

I was glad of an opportunity of hearing both the South Carolina senators, soon after my arrival in Washington. They are listened to with close attention; and every indication of their state of feeling is watched with the interest which has survived the Nullification struggle. Mr. Calhoun on this occasion let us a little into his mind; Mr. Preston kept more closely to the question before the body. The question was whether a vote of censure of the President, recorded in the minutes of the proceedings of the Senate, the preceding session, should be expunged. The motion for the expunging was made by Colonel Benton, and rejected, as it had been before, and has been since; though it was finally carried, to the agony of the opposition, at the end of last session, (February, 1837.)

Mr. Preston was out of health, and unable to throw his accustomed force into his speaking; but his effort showed us how beautiful his eloquence is in its way. It is not solid. His speeches, if taken to pieces, will be found to consist of analogies and declamation; but his figures are sometimes very striking, and his manner is as graceful as anything so artificial can be. I never before understood the eloquence of action. The action of public speakers in England, as far as I have observed, (and perhaps I may be allowed to hint that deaf persons are peculiarly qualified to judge of the nature of such action) is of two kinds,—the involuntary gesture which is resorted to for the relief of the nerves, which may or may not be expressive of meaning; and the action which is wholly the result of study,— arbitrary and not the birth of the sentiment; and therefore, though pleasing perhaps to the eye, per- plexing to the mind of the listener. Mr. Preston's manner unites the advantages of these two methods, and avoids most of their evils. It is easy to see that he could not speak without an abundant use of action; and that he has therefore done wisely in making it a study. To an unaccustomed eye it appears somewhat exuberant; but it is exquisitely graceful, and far more than commonly appropriate. His voice is not good, but his person is tall, stout and commanding, and his countenance animated.

Mr. Calhoun followed, and impressed me very strongly. While he kept to the question, what he said was close, good, and moderate, though delivered in rapid speech, and with a voice not sufficiently modulated. But when he began to reply to a taunt of Colonel Benton's, that he wanted to be President, the force of his speaking became painful. He made protestations which it seemed to strangers had better have been spared, that he would not turn on his heel to be President; and that he had given up all for his own brave, magnanimous little State of South Carolina. While thus protesting, his eyes flashed, his brow seemed charged with thunder, his voice became almost a bark, and his sentences were abrupt, intense, producing in the auditory that sort of laugh which is squeezed out of people by the application of a very sudden mental force. I believe he little knew what a revelation he made in a few sentences. They were to us strangers the key,

not only to all that was said and done by the South
Carolina party during the remainder of the session,
but to many things at Charleston and Columbia,
which would otherwise have passed unobserved or
unexplained.

I was less struck than some strangers appear to
have been with the length and prosy character of
the speeches in Congress. I do not remember
hearing any senator (always excepting Colonel Benton) speak for more than an hour. I was seldom
present in the other House, where probably the
most diffuse oratory is heard; but I was daily informed of the proceedings there, by the representative who was of our party; and I did not find that
there was much annoyance or delay from this cause.
Perhaps the practice may be connected with the
amount of business to be done. It is well known
that the business of Congress is so moderate in
quantity, from the functions of the general Government being few and simple, that it would be considered a mere trifle by any parliament in the Old
World: and long speeches which would be a great
annoyance elsewhere may be an innocent pastime
in an assembly which may have leisure upon its
hands.

The gallery of the splendid Hall of Representatives is not well contrived for hearing; and I rarely
went into it for more than a passing view of what

was going on : a view which might be taken without disturbance to anybody, as the gallery was generally empty, and too high raised above the area of the hall, to fix the eye of the members. My chief interest was watching Mr. Adams, of whose speaking, however, I can give no account. The circumstance of this gentleman being now a member of the representative body after having been President, fixes the attention of all Europeans upon him, with as much admiration as interest. He is one of the most remarkable men in America. He is an embodiment of the pure, simple morals which are assumed to prevail in the thriving young republic. His term of office was marked by nothing so much as by the subordination of glory to goodness,—of showy objects to moral ones. The eccentricity of thought and action in Mr. Adams, of which his admirers bitterly or sorrowfully complain, and which renders him an impracticable member of a party, arises from the same honest simplicity which crowns his virtues, mingled with a faulty taste and an imperfect temper. His hastiness of assertion has sometimes placed him in predicaments so undignified as almost to be a set-off against the honours he wins by pertinacious and bold adherence to a principle which he considers sound. His occasional starts out of the ranks of his party, without notice, and without apparent cause, have been in vain attempted to be

explained on suppositions of interest or vanity : they
may be more easily accounted for in other ways.
Between one day and another, some new idea of
justice and impartiality may strike his brain, and
send him to the House warm with invective against
his party, and sympathy with their foes. He rises,
and speaks out all his new mind, to the perplexity
of the whole assembly, every man of whom bends
to hear every syllable he says,—perplexity which
gives way to dismay on the one hand and triumph
on the other. The triumphant party begins to coax
and honour him ; but before the process is well begun, he is off again, finding that he had gone too
far ; and the probability is that he finishes by placing
himself between two fires. I now describe what I
actually witnessed of his conduct in one instance ;
conduct which left no more doubt of his integrity
than of his eccentricity. He was well described to
me before I saw him. " Study Mr. Adams," was
the exhortation. " You will find him well worth
it. He runs in veins ; if you light upon one, you
will find him marvellously rich ; if not, you may
chance to meet rubbish. In action, he is very peculiar. He will do ninety-nine things nobly,—
excellently ;—but the hundredth will be so bad in
taste and temper, that it will drive all the rest out
of your head, if you don't take care." His countrymen will " take care." Whatever the heats of

party may be, however the tone of disappointment against Mr. Adams may sometimes rise to something too like hatred, there is undoubtedly a deep reverence and affection for the man in the nation's heart; and any one may safely prophecy that his reputation, half a century after his death, will be of a very honourable kind. He fought a stout and noble battle in Congress last session in favour of discussion of the Slavery question, and in defence of the right of petition upon it,—on behalf of women as well as of men. While hunted, held at bay, almost torn to pieces by an outrageous majority,—leaving him, I believe, in absolute unity,—he preserved a boldness and coolness as amusing as they were admirable. Though he now and then vents his spleen with violence when disappointed in a favourite object, he seems able to bear perfectly well that which it is the great fault of Americans to shrink from,—singularity and blame. He seems at times reckless of opinion; and this is the point of his character which his countrymen seem, naturally, least able to comprehend.

Such is the result of the observations I was able to make on this gentleman when at Washington. I was prevented seeing so much of him as I earnestly desired by his family circumstances. He had just lost a son, and did not appear in society. It is well known in America that Mr. Adams will leave be-

hind him papers of inestimable value. For forty
years (I was told) he has kept a diary, full and
exact. In this diary he every morning sets down
not only the events of the preceding day, but. the
conversations he has had with foreigners, and on all
subjects of interest. This immense accumulation
of papers will afford such materials for history as
the country has never yet been blessed with. Perhaps no country has ever possessed a public man,
of great powers, and involved in all the remarkable
events of its most remarkable period, who has had
industry enough to leave behind him a similar record
of his times. This will probably turn out to be
(whether he thinks so or not) the greatest and most
useful of his deeds, and his most honourable monument.

Those whose taste is the contemplation of great
and original men, may always have it gratified by
going to Washington. Whatever may be thought
of the form and administration of government there,
—however certain it may be that the greatest men
are not, in this age of the world, to be found in
political life,—it cannot be but that among the real
representatives of a composite and self-governing
nation, there must be many men of power,—power
of intellect, of goodness, or, at least, of will.

MOUNT VERNON.

"He might have been a king
But that he understood
How much it was a meaner thing
To be unjustly great than honorably good."
Duke of Buckingham on Lord Fairfax.

On the 2nd of February, I visited Mount Vernon, in company with a large party of gentlemen and ladies. Of all places in America, the family seat and burial place of Washington is that which strangers are most eager to visit. I was introduced by Judge Story to the resident family, and was received by them, with all my companions, with great civility and kindness.

The estate of Mount Vernon was inherited by General Washington from his brother. For fifteen years prior to the assembling of the first general Congress in Philadelphia, Washington spent his time chiefly on this property, repairing to the provincial legislature when duty called him there, but gladly returning to the improvement of his lands. The house was, in those days, a very modest building, consisting of only four rooms on a floor, which form the centre of the present mansion. Mrs.

Washington resided there during the ten years' absence of her husband, in the wars of the Revolution; repairing to head-quarters at the close of each campaign, and remaining there till the opening of the next. The departure of an aide-de-camp from the camp, to escort the general's lady, was watched for with much anxiety, as the echoes of the last shot of the campaign died away; for the arrival of " Lady Washington" (as the soldiers called her) was the signal for the wives of all the general officers to repair to their husbands in camp. A sudden cheerfulness diffused itself through the army when the plain chariot, with the postilions in their scarlet and white liveries, was seen to stop before the general's door. Mrs. Washington was wont to say, in her latter years, that she had heard the first cannon at the opening, and the last at the close of every campaign of the revolutionary war. She was a strong-minded, even-tempered woman; and the cheerfulness of her demeanour, under the heavy and various anxieties of such a lot as hers, was no mean support to her husband's spirits, and to the bravery and hopefulness of the whole army, whose eyes were fixed upon her. She retired from amidst the homage of the camp with serene composure, when the fatigues and perils of warfare had to be resumed, and hid her fears and cares in her retired home. There she occupied herself industriously in

the superintendence of her slaves, and in striving to
stop the ravages which her husband's public service
was making in his private fortunes.

After the peace of 1783, she was joined by her
husband, who made a serious pursuit of laying out
gardens and grounds round his dwelling, and building large additions to it. He then enjoyed only
four years of quiet, being called in 1787 to preside
in the convention which framed the Constitution;
and in 1789 to fill the Presidential chair. Mrs.
Washington was now obliged to quit the estate with
him ; and it was eight years before they could take
possession of it again. In 1797 Washington refused to be made President for a third term, and
retired into as private a life as it was possible for
him to secure. Trains of visitors sought him in
his retreat, and Mrs. Washington's accomplish-
ments as a Virginian housewife were found useful
every day : but Washington was at home, and he
was happy. In a little while he was once more
applied to to serve the State at the head of her
armies. He did not refuse, but requested to be
left in peace till there should be actual want of his
presence. Before that time arrived he was no more.
Two years after his retirement, while the sense of
enjoyment of repose was still fresh, and his mind
was full of such schemes as delight the imaginations of country gentlemen, death overtook him,

and found him, though the call was somewhat sudden, ready and willing to go. In a little more than two years he was followed by his wife. From the appearance of the estate, it would seem to have been going to decay ever since.

Our party, in three carriages, and five or six on horseback, left Washington about nine o'clock, and reached Alexandria in an hour and a half, though our passage over the long bridge which crosses the Potomac was very slow, from its being in a sad state of dilapidation. Having ordered a late dinner at Alexandria, we proceeded on our way, occasionally looking behind us at the great dome of the Capitol, still visible above the low hills which border the grey, still Potomac, now stretching cold amidst the wintry landscape. It was one of the coldest days I ever felt; the bitter wind seeming to eat into one's very life. The last five miles of the eight which lie between Alexandria and Mount Vernon wound through the shelter of the woods, so that we recovered a little from the extreme cold before we reached the house. The land appears to be quite impoverished; the fences and gates are in bad order; much of the road was swampy, and the poor young lambs, shivering in the biting wind, seemed to look round in vain for shelter and care. The conservatories were almost in ruins, scarcely a single pane of glass being unbroken; and the house

looked as if it had not been painted on the outside
for years. Little negroes peeped at us from behind
the pillars of the piazza as we drove up. We
alighted in silence, most of us being probably occupied with the thought of who had been there before
us,—what crowds of the noble, the wise, the good
had come hither to hear the yet living voice of the
most unimpeachable of patriots! As I looked up,
I almost expected to see him standing in the doorway. My eyes had rested on the image of his
remarkable countenance in almost every house I
had entered; and here, in his own dwelling, one
could not but look for the living face with something more than the eye of the imagination. I
cared far less for any of the things that were shown
me within the house than to stay in the piazza next
the garden, and fancy how he here walked in meditation, or stood looking abroad over the beautiful
river, and pleasing his eye with a far different spectacle from that of camps and conventions.

Many prints of British landscapes, residences,
and events, are hung up in the apartments. The
ponderous key of the Bastille still figures in the
hall, in extraordinary contrast with everything else
in this republican residence. The Bible in the
library is the only book of Washington's now left.
The best likeness of the great man, known to all
travellers from the oddness of the material on which

it is preserved, is to be seen here, sanctioned thus by the testimony of the family. The best likeness of Washington happens to be on a common pitcher. As soon as this was discovered, the whole edition of pitchers was bought up. Once or twice I saw the entire vessel, locked up in a cabinet, or in some such way secured from accident: but most of its possessors have, like the family, cut out the portrait, and had it framed.

The walk, planned and partly finished during Washington's life,—the winding path on the verge of the green slope above the river, must be very sweet in summer. The beauty of the situation of the place surprised me. The river was nobler, the terrace finer, and the swelling hills around more varied than I had imagined ; but there is a painful air of desolation over the whole. I wonder how it struck the British officers in 1814, when, in passing up the river on their bandit expedition to burn libraries and bridges, and raze senate chambers, they assembled on deck, and uncovered their heads as they passed the silent dwelling of the great man who was not there to testify his disgust at the service they were upon. If they knew what it was that they were under orders to do, it would have been creditable to them as men to have mutinied in front of Mount Vernon.

The old tomb from which the body of Washing-

ton has been removed ought to be obliterated or
restored. It is too painful to see it as it is now,—
the brickwork mouldering, and the paling broken
and scattered. The red cedars still overshadow it;
and it is a noble resting-place. Every one would
mourn to see the low house destroyed, and the great
man's chamber of dreamless sleep made no longer
sacred from the common tread: but anything is
better than the air of neglect which now wounds the
spirit of the pilgrim. The body lies, with that of
Judge Washington, in a vault near, in a more
secluded, but far less beautiful situation than that
on the verge of the Potomac. The river is not
seen from the new vault; and the erection is very
sordid. It is of red brick, with an iron door, and
looks more like an oven than anything else, except
for the stone slab, bearing a funereal text, which is
inserted over the door. The bank which rises on
one side is planted with cedars, pines, and a sprinkling of beech and birch, so that the vault is overshadowed in summer, as the places of the dead
should be. The President told me that the desolation about the tomb was a cause of uneasiness to
himself and many others; and that he had urged
the family, as the body had been already removed
from its original bed, to permit it to be interred in
the centre of the Capitol. They very naturally
cling to the precious possession; and there is

certainly something much more accordant with the spirit of the man in a grave under the trees of his own home than in a magnificent shrine : but, however modest the tomb may be,—were it only such a green hillock as every rustic lies under,—it should bear tokens of reverent care. The grass and shade which he so much loved are the only ornaments needed ; the absence of all that can offend the eye and hurt the spirit of reverence, is all that the patriot and the pilgrim require.

Before we reached the crazy bridge, which it had been difficult enough to pass in the morning, the sweet Potomac lay in clear moonshine, and the lights round the Capitol twinkled from afar. On arriving at our fireside, we found how delightful a total change of mood sometimes is. Tea, letters, and English newspapers awaited us : and they were a surprising solace, chilled or feverish as we were with the intense cold and strong mental excitement of the day.